New Directions for
Teaching and Learning

Catherine M. Wehlburg
EDITOR-IN-CHIEF

Discipline-Centered Learning Communities: Creating Connections Among Students, Faculty, and Curricula

Kimberly Buch
Kenneth E. Barron
EDITORS

Number 132 • Winter 2012
Jossey-Bass
San Francisco

DISCIPLINE-CENTERED LEARNING COMMUNITIES: CREATING
CONNECTIONS AMONG STUDENTS, FACULTY, AND CURRICULA
Kimberly Buch, Kenneth E. Barron (eds.)
New Directions for Teaching and Learning, no. 132
Catherine M. Wehlburg, Editor-in-Chief

Microfilm copies of issues and articles are available in 16mm and 35mm,
as well as microfiche in 105mm, through University Microfilms, Inc.,
300 North Zeeb Road, Ann Arbor, MI 48106-1346.

NEW DIRECTIONS FOR TEACHING AND LEARNING (ISSN 0271-0633, elec-
tronic ISSN 1536-0768) is part of The Jossey-Bass Higher and Adult
Education Series and is published quarterly by Wiley Subscription
Services, Inc., A Wiley Company, at Jossey-Bass, One Montgomery Street,
Suite 1200, San Francisco, CA 94104-4594. Periodicals postage paid at
San Francisco, CA, and at additional mailing offices. POSTMASTER:
Send address changes to New Directions for Teaching and Learning,
Jossey-Bass, One Montgomery Street, Suite 1200, San Francisco, CA
94104-4594.

New Directions for Teaching and Learning is indexed in CIJE: Current
Index to Journals in Education (ERIC), Contents Pages in Education
(T&F), Educational Research Abstracts Online (T&F), ERIC Database
(Education Resources Information Center), Higher Education Abstracts
(Claremont Graduate University), and SCOPUS (Elsevier).

INDIVIDUAL SUBSCRIPTION RATE (in USD): $89 per year US/Can/Mex, $113
rest of world; institutional subscription rate: $292 US, $332 Can/Mex, $366
rest of world. Single copy rate: $29. Electronic only–all regions: $89
individual, $292 institutional; Print & Electronic–US: $98 individual,
$335 institutional; Print & Electronic–Canada/Mexico: $98 individual,
$375 institutional; Print & Electronic–Rest of World: $122 individual, $409
institutional.

EDITORIAL CORRESPONDENCE should be sent to the editor-in-chief,
Catherine M. Wehlburg, c.wehlburg@tcu.edu.

www.josseybass.com

Contents

FROM THE SERIES EDITOR

About This Publication

Since 1980, *New Directions for Teaching and Learning* (NDTL) has brought a unique blend of theory, research, and practice to leaders in postsecondary education. *NDTL* sourcebooks strive not only for solid substance but also for timeliness, compactness, and accessibility.

The series has four goals: to inform readers about current and future directions in teaching and learning in postsecondary education, to illuminate the context that shapes these new directions, to illustrate these new directions through examples from real settings, and to propose ways in which these new directions can be incorporated into still other settings.

This publication reflects the view that teaching deserves respect as a high form of scholarship. We believe that significant scholarship is conducted not only by researchers who report results of empirical investigations but also by practitioners who share disciplinary reflections about teaching. Contributors to *NDTL* approach questions of teaching and learning as seriously as they approach substantive questions in their own disciplines, and they deal not only with pedagogical issues but also with the intellectual and social context in which these issues arise. Authors deal on the one hand with theory and research and on the other with practice, and they translate from research and theory to practice and back again.

About This Volume

Discipline-Centered Learning Communities: Creating Connections Among Students, Faculty, and Curricula describes and reflects the changing uses of learning communities in higher education focusing on discipline-centered communities. This issue is a resource for those who work with or are interested in learning communities as it provides not just models of what is working but also abundant resources and future directions for this educational approach. Focusing on the academic discipline of psychology, the authors provide a reflective and exciting approach to the development and use of learning communities.

Catherine M. Wehlburg
Editor-in-Chief

CATHERINE M. WEHLBURG is the assistant provost for institutional effectiveness at Texas Christian University.

EDITORS' NOTES

We set out with several goals for this volume. First, we wanted to extend the existing learning community literature by presenting an *intradisciplinary* perspective as a complement to the *interdisciplinary* perspective traditionally used in discussions of learning communities in higher education. We certainly appreciate the interdisciplinary perspective, and have seen learning communities used as an effective vehicle for interdisciplinary curricular reform and student engagement at our own institutions. At the same time, we have also observed an increasing use of learning communities as vehicles for achieving departmental or program-specific goals and enhancing major-specific or discipline-specific student learning outcomes. Learning communities at our own institutions have followed a similar developmental pattern, beginning with general education-based learning communities for undeclared students and expanding in the direction of discipline-centered learning communities for students interested in particular majors. Currently, over half of the learning communities at our two institutions are centered within a discipline. As faculty members who developed discipline-centered learning communities in our own departments, we have been a part of this evolution.

Thus, we offer the current volume hoping to carry forward the work begun two decades ago in another New Directions volume, *Learning Communities: Creating Connections Among Students, Faculty, and Disciplines*. Its authors—Faith Gabelnick, Jean MacGregor, Roberta Matthews, and Barbara Leigh Smith—inspired many faculty, staff, and administrators to join the learning community movement by showing their potential for creating connections among students, faculty, and curricula *across disciplines*. And, as indicated by our title, we have found learning communities to be a powerful vehicle for creating connections among students, faculty, and curricula *within a discipline* as well.

However, this evolution has brought new conditions and challenges, along with a new audience of faculty and administrator stakeholders. Thus, our second goal for this volume is to provide a useful resource for these stakeholders. We have met many faculty and department chairs who want to learn more about the viability and versatility of creating learning communities in their departments; they are asking about their potential benefits, required resources, and common challenges. We also have been asked about the nuts and bolts of designing, implementing, and evaluating

NEW DIRECTIONS FOR TEACHING AND LEARNING, no. 132, Winter 2012 © Wiley Periodicals, Inc.
Published online in Wiley Online Library (wileyonlinelibrary.com) • DOI: 10.1002/tl.20031

discipline-centered learning communities. We hope this volume will provide practical answers to these questions as well as links to additional resources to help others create similar initiatives in their departments and disciplines.

Our third goal is to highlight another evolution of the learning community movement that offers alternative definitions and new models on how to promote learning communities. Anne Goodsell Love, a contemporary leader in this movement, has contributed an introductory chapter on the background, growth, and evolution of learning communities. Part of this evolution is a broad view of learning communities that includes not just the traditional curriculum-based approach but also communities based within a classroom, communities defined by student organizations, and communities enabled by virtual connections. In 1999, Lenning and Ebbers proposed a typology of learning communities that recognized all of these as vehicles for creating connections that may lead to desired academic outcomes. We have used Lenning and Ebbers's typology—which includes curriculum-based, residential-based, classroom-based, student-based, and virtual-based learning communities—to structure the current volume.

We have recruited faculty from one particular discipline—psychology —to showcase how all five types of learning communities can be created to enhance student engagement. Specifically, Chapters Two and Three describe different approaches for creating curriculum-based learning communities within the discipline of psychology. In Chapter Two, Mark Zrull, Courtney Rocheleau, Corinne Smith, and Shawn Bergman describe the Brain Matters learning community that they offer for first-year students at Appalachian State University, and in Chapter Three Laurence Nolan and Steve Jenkins describe Psychology: Then and Now, a capstone LC for seniors at Wagner College. Chapter Four features a residential-based learning community at Loyola Marymount University, The Psychology Early Awareness Program (PEAP), developed by authors Cheryl Grills, Adam Fingerhut, Vandana Thadani, and Ricardo Arturo Machón. In Chapter Five, Bryan Saville, Natalie Kerr Lawrence, and Krisztina Jakobsen describe how they create learning communities within a wide range of undergraduate and graduate psychology classrooms at James Madison University, using a variety of active learning strategies. In Chapter Six, Michael Hall describes how a discipline-centered student organization—in this case, Psi Chi, the international honor society in psychology—can be the foundation for a student-based learning community within a major. Although not included as an existing type of learning community in the 1999 typology, Lenning and Ebbers predicted that virtual learning communities had great potential for the future. The past decade has supported their prediction, and in Chapter Seven, Anita Blanchard and James Cook of the University of North Carolina Charlotte describe the potential for virtual learning communities to make connections among students and curricula and for supplementing the other types of learning communities described in Chapters Two through

Six. In Chapter Eight, we are delighted to end the volume with a retrospective chapter by three of the original learning community pioneers—Roberta Matthews, Barbara Leigh Smith, and Jean MacGregor.

Although Lenning and Ebbers's typology can help illustrate the variety and versatility of learning communities, we also acknowledge that any typology can create the appearance of artificial boundaries between different types of learning communities. For example, although an initiative may be classified as a residential-based learning community because of its residential component, most are also combined with a strong curricular component. Similarly, although we intentionally focused the book's examples on one particular discipline to showcase how all five types of learning communities can be applied to psychology, we intend the content to be generalizable to learning communities centered in any discipline in higher education. Toward that end, we provide an appendix of additional learning community resources with a comprehensive list of example learning communities from a wide array of other disciplines. We hope readers walk away inspired by the rich variety and vast versatility of learning communities and how they might be used within their own disciplines and academic programs.

Kimberly Buch
Kenneth E. Barron
Editors

Reference

Lenning, O. T., and Ebbers, L. H. *The Powerful Potential of Learning Communities: Improving Education for the Future.* ASHE-ERIC Higher Education Report, Vol. 26, No. 6. Washington, D. C.: Graduate School of Education and Human Development, George Washington University, 1999.

KIMBERLY BUCH *is professor of psychology and coordinator of the Psychology Learning Community at the University of North Carolina Charlotte.*

KENNETH E. BARRON *is professor of psychology and coordinator of the Psychology Learning Community at James Madison University.*

1

Learning communities carry on a tradition of educational reform, resulting in improved student learning outcomes.

The Growth and Current State of Learning Communities in Higher Education

Anne Goodsell Love

Learning Communities and Student Engagement

Over the past two decades, growth in learning communities (LCs) has increased steadily on college campuses (Barefoot, 2002; Smith and MacGregor, 2009). Colleges and universities of all sizes and types now implement LCs for some or all of their students, usually with the aim of improving student learning, improving students' experiences in and out of the classroom, providing integration of ideas and disciplines to combat increasing specialization and compartmentalization of disciplines, and increasing rates of student retention and degree completion. As the cost of higher education soars so have expectations for student success, and calls for undergraduate education reform appear on a regular basis. LCs are one reform effort to change how students, faculty, and student affairs professionals work together to form a more holistic learning experience, both across and within disciplines.

LCs put theory into practice by leveraging a number of components crucial to student learning and development. Alexander Astin and his colleagues at UCLA studied college students for decades and summarized much of their research this way: "The single most important environmental influence on student development is the peer group. By judicious and imaginative use of peer groups, any college or university can substantially strengthen its impact on student learning and personal development"

New Directions for Teaching and Learning, no. 132, Winter 2012 © Wiley Periodicals, Inc.
Published online in Wiley Online Library (wileyonlinelibrary.com) • DOI: 10.1002/tl.20032

(Astin, 1993, p. xxii). A second influence on student learning and development is the frequency of interaction with faculty, and a third influence is the degree to which students are actively engaged and are willing to put in time and effort in learning (Astin, 1993).

In a similar vein, Vincent Tinto at Syracuse University has led the scholarship on student retention, and his search to find factors that were fundamental to increasing student retention led him to LCs. Briefly, Tinto's theory is that students' social and intellectual integration into the academic and social communities of college are essential factors in determining whether students will stay in college and complete their degrees (Tinto, 1987). Tinto's research on LCs demonstrated that, with their attention to learning (the intellectual integration and development) *and* community (the social realm or context in which the learning is embedded), LCs were effective in linking the social and academic lives of students (Tinto, Goodsell, and Russo, 1994).

Inspired by C. Robert Pace's earlier research that linked the "quality of student effort" with increases in student achievement (Pace, 1979), George Kuh and his colleagues at Indiana University have examined student engagement extensively and in doing so developed the National Survey of Student Engagement ("NSSE Home," n.d.). *Student Success in College: Creating Conditions that Matter* (Kuh, Kinzie, Schuh, and Whitt, 2005) is a culmination of this research, and it begins with this assertion:

> What students *do* in college counts more in terms of what they learn and whether they will persist in college than who they are or even where they go to college. That is, the voluminous research on college student development shows that the time and energy students devote to educationally purposeful activities is the single best predictor of their learning and personal development. (Kuh and others, 2005, p. 8)

They conclude that the two key components of student engagement that contribute to student success are "the amount of time and effort students put into their studies and other activities that lead to the experiences and outcomes that constitute student success... and the ways the institution allocates resources and organizes learning opportunities and services to induce students to participate in and benefit from such activities" (Kuh and others, 2005, p. 9). They call educational programs and practices that incorporate these components "high-impact" practices and cite LCs as one example.

A further reference in making the case for the need to maximize student engagement are the "Seven Principles for Good Practice in Undergraduate Education," which list factors highly correlated with high levels of student engagement (Chickering and Gamson, 1987). The seven principles are student-faculty contact, cooperation among students, active learning, prompt feedback, time on task, high expectations, and respect for diverse talents and ways of learning. Many programs have been developed on campuses in response to these theories, principles, and calls for action. LCs provide a unifying construct that includes students, faculty, and other campus professionals in ways that incorporate these theories and principles on campuses.

More information to support the development of LCs on campus is found in *Creating Learning Communities: A Practical Guide to Winning Support, Organizing for Change, and Implementing Programs* (Shapiro and Levine, 1999). Their follow-up book, *Sustaining and Improving Learning Communities* (Levine Laufgraben and Shapiro, 2004) reinforces the need for LCs and expands on planning and assessment, faculty development, approaching diversity through learning communities, and living–learning programs.

Definitions of Learning Communities

The term "learning community" is ubiquitous in higher education, sometimes referring to on-line courses, on-campus living arrangements, faculty research groups, or colleges and universities as a whole. Responding to calls for improvement in higher education in the 1990s, the Boyer Commission urged research universities to "foster a community of learners" (Boyer Commission on Educating Undergraduates in the Research University, 1998, p. 34). A monograph at about the same time defined an LC as "an intentionally developed community that will promote and maximize learning" (Lenning and Ebbers, 1999, p. 8) and proposed a typology of LCs that is used in this volume: curricular LCs (interdisciplinary or intradisciplinary, across classes), classroom LCs (within singular courses), residential LCs, student-type LCs (for different demographic groups of students or students with similar interests), and virtual LCs (Lenning and Ebbers, 1999, p. 10).

As LCs have developed, the term most commonly is associated with an intentional restructuring of the curriculum and student course-taking patterns to emphasize an interdisciplinary focus with attention paid to students' academic and social development. Long-time practitioners and champions of LCs Barbara Leigh Smith, Jean MacGregor, Roberta Matthews, and Faith Gabelnick put it this way:

> Learning communities are a variety of curricular approaches that intentionally link or cluster two or more courses, often around an interdisciplinary theme or problem, and enroll a common cohort of students. This represents an intentional restructuring of students' time, credit, and learning experiences to build community, enhance learning, and foster connections among students, faculty, and disciplines. At their best, learning communities practice pedagogies of active engagement and reflection. (Smith, MacGregor, Matthews, and Gabelnick, 2004, p. 67)

To illustrate these various definitions, the following is a description of LCs at Wagner College, where more than one type of LC is embedded into the undergraduate curriculum. Wagner College created the Wagner Plan for the Practical Liberal Arts in 1998, with LCs and experiential learning (including service learning and civic engagement) as centerpieces of the undergraduate curriculum (Guarasci, 2006). The program "is designed to put students into their surrounding environment and to understand the practical applications of their learning throughout their Wagner experience" (Smith and MacGregor, 2009, p. 129). Enactment of this change required active involvement on the part of the faculty, most of whom were energized by the collaborative work of creating the new curriculum. All students enroll in an LC in their first semester (First-Year Program, FYP), in their intermediate years (ILC), and in the senior year (SLC). The FYP and ILC emphasize interdisciplinary learning, whereas the SLC is an intra-disciplinary combination of two courses in the major. The FYP and SLC incorporate experiential learning, civic engagement, and reflective writing in a discipline. Integration of in-class and out-of-class learning continues beyond courses, as the administrative–student affairs focus has shifted from student activities to cocurricular programs, including efforts to internationalize and diversify not just the curriculum but the campus as a whole.

The Wagner Plan also demonstrates the intentional implementation of what Smith and others refer to as LC core practices: "community, diversity, integration, active learning, and reflection/assessment" (Smith and others, 2004, p. 97). These core practices echo the theories cited previously, and help to explain the power of LCs. By addressing a number of factors that are key to enhancing student engagement and learning, LCs can reinforce and build upon the gains of each factor, potentially making the whole of the LC experience greater than the sum of its parts.

Learning Community Growth and Expansion

Most of the literature about LCs traces its roots to the 1920s and the work of John Dewey and Alexander Meiklejohn (Gabelnick, MacGregor, Matthews, and Smith, 1990; Shapiro and Levine, 1999; Smith and others, 2004). Both founded experimental schools—Dewey, an elementary school; Meiklejohn, the Experimental College within the University of Wisconsin—where they could put into practice their theories about learning as a social process. Both incorporated active learning into the design of the curriculum, believing that student interaction with each other, their teachers, and their community was an essential way to place education into a democratic context (Smith and others, 2004). For example, among the innovations of Meiklejohn's Experimental College was a required research project to be done by students during the summer between their freshman and sophomore years. Students used their hometowns as laboratories, examining various sociological and political patterns, and applying the theories they had been learning in the classroom to the "real world" environments around them.

Another of Meiklejohn's legacies that became manifested in LCs was the emphasis on integration of ideas across disciplines and restructuring the curriculum across courses and semesters. The Experimental College was a lower-division academic program, encompassing the first two years of study at the university, and instead of the series of separate elective courses that non–Experimental College students followed, students in the Experimental College took an integrated program of study, what we now would call an LC (Smith and others, 2004). In addition, students in the Experimental College lived together in a residence hall, as the design of the college included students' social networks that would reinforce academic habits and culture (Smith and others, 2004). In Meiklejohn's Experimental College can be seen the precursors to living–learning communities, LCs with experiential or service learning, and LCs with a common theme and interdisciplinary teaching, such as clusters and coordinated studies programs, that aim to transcend individual courses.

The rapid expansion of higher education in the 1960s and 1970s included the development of innovative curricular structures and programs that clustered courses, faculty, and students in ways designed to foster community, increase curricular coherence and integration, and retain a balance of education for the public good (the commitment to democratic education championed by Dewey and Meiklejohn) and education for workforce development (as community colleges were being created to do) (Smith and others, 2004). Among the innovations were subcolleges within universities, such as honors colleges, and integrated academic programs for first- and second-year students. One such innovation was created in the mid-1960s, an "Experimental Program" at the University of California at Berkeley (Smith and others, 2004; Tussman, 1969). Joseph Tussman, a professor at Berkeley (who was a student of Meiklejohn at the University of Wisconsin but after the Experimental College had ended) and his colleagues endeavored to address what they saw as the problem of the tug-of-war between the purposes of a university (the generation of new knowledge) and a college (the cultivation of minds). Making the argument that a focus on individual courses contributes to overall curricular disintegration, Tussman wrote about the fragmentation of the efforts of professors and students, concluding that "the effect is that no teacher is in a position to be responsible for, or effectively concerned with, the student's total educational situation. The student presents himself to the teacher in fragments, and not even the advising system can put him together again" (Tussman, 1969, p. 6). He goes on to advocate for a two-year lower division educational program with a comprehensive, interdisciplinary scope and interrelated responsibilities for teachers. The Experimental Program stood somewhat outside the rest of the university and lasted for three years, but like its predecessor the Experimental College, its restructuring and integration of courses within and across semesters sought to bring community and coherence to the experiences of students and faculty in much the same way as current LCs.

There is more to the history and development of LCs, and much of it is captured in *Learning Communities: Reforming Undergraduate Education* (Smith and others, 2004). To paraphrase a summary of these reforms and the educational theories they embrace, "Learning communities are the pedagogical embodiment of the belief that teaching and learning are relational processes, involving co-creating knowledge through relationships among students, between students and teachers, and through the environment in which these relationships operate" (Price, 2005, p. 6).

The Current State of Learning Communities

LCs are found at all types of colleges and universities, and at all levels of courses, from developmental to graduate. Learning community growth has increased steadily since their adoption in the early 1970s by a few colleges and universities—SUNY Stony Brook (New York), LaGuardia Community College (New York), and the Evergreen State College (Washington), among the earliest—to their presence at more than 800 colleges and universities (Smith and MacGregor, 2009, p. 120). According to the National Survey of Student Engagement (NSSE), in 2002, 30 percent of first-year students and 23 percent of seniors at four-year colleges or universities participating in the survey were in an LC or planned to be in one (Zhao and Kuh, 2004, p. 120). Students were evenly represented at public and private institutions (Zhao and Kuh, 2004, p. 122). The Policy Center on the First Year of College reported that approximately 62 percent of colleges enrolled at least some first-year students into learning communities; LCs were most common at research-extensive universities (present at 82 percent) and least common at small baccalaureate colleges (present at 46 percent) (Barefoot, 2002). Of the 298 colleges and universities listed in the LC directory on the National Learning Commons website, approximately 39 percent are community colleges and 61 percent are baccalaureate-degree (or higher degree) granting institutions ("National Learning Communities Directory Search," n.d.).

The Impact of Learning Communities

LCs have grown rapidly, and anecdotal reports attest to their popularity, but what research demonstrates their effectiveness? This section reviews literature on the impact of LCs, highlighting a sample of single-institution studies and describing results from multi-institutional studies. For a comprehensive review of LC research prior to 2003, see the monograph *Learning Community Research and Assessment: What We Know Now* (Taylor, Moore, MacGregor, and Lindblad, 2003). As with LCs themselves, the reports reviewed varied substantially, examining outcomes such as grades,

NEW DIRECTIONS FOR TEACHING AND LEARNING • DOI: 10.1002/tl

course completion, students' perceptions of their experiences, retention in college, and graduation. Information is included from journal articles, dissertations, unpublished reports, conference presentations, and granting agency reports. Although it was difficult to compare directly such varied data, the researchers concluded that "those studies that looked at retention, academic success, and satisfaction reported overwhelmingly positive results. These findings held without regard to the size of the study or the type of the learning community undertaken, suggesting that even modest learning community initiatives are likely to reap positive outcomes" (Taylor and others, 2003, p. 19).

The *Journal of Learning Community Research*, first published in 2006, has added to the number of studies available about LCs (rather than relying on campus reports or conference presentations). Articles include research reports, case studies, descriptions of program implementation and revision, and book reviews. A number of studies have examined LCs in specific courses or disciplines. For example, faculty at the University of North Carolina at Charlotte who implemented and assessed LCs for first-year psychology majors over four years found that students in the LC achieved the program goals at significantly higher rates than their non-LC peers (Buch and Spaulding, 2008). Specifically, small cohorts of students in the LC taking courses together with advising by one of the LC faculty achieved higher grade point averages (GPAs) and one-year retention rates than the non-LC control group, which was matched statistically for ethnicity, SAT scores, and predicted GPA. In addition, students in the LC made more timely progress toward degree and more timely completion of an upper-level research methods course that is a gateway course for other upper-level major courses. Assessment of student achievement and other program goals continued beyond the year that the students were in the LC, demonstrating more than a one-semester or one-year impact of the LC.

Students at Dickinson College were surveyed and participated in focus groups for four years to assess the impact of LCs on students' engaged learning, civic development, and well-being (Finley, 2009). LCs at Dickinson involved a first-year seminar in which the faculty member was the advisor for the students in the course, and the course included required out-of-class experiences (assorted meals, attendance at guest lectures, events, and so on). Students who were not in an LC took a first-year seminar without the related advising and cocurricular components. "Overall, the trend effect . . . suggests that LC students are learning in different ways and engaging in ostensibly deeper levels than students in stand-alone seminars" (Finley, 2009, p. 5). The factors associated with this trend were described by students and included the importance of reflection on the outside experiences, and active participation in experiences that allowed students to apply what they were learning in the classroom. Students in stand-alone seminars talked about engagement in the course being related to the performance of the seminar instructor, their own interest in the course, or seeing the course as a requirement to fulfill. Results related to student well-being showed significantly lower levels of alcohol consumption among students who had been in an LC; these lower levels were consistent across the four years. "The qualitative data suggest this finding may be an artifact of the social climate created by LCs," as students discussed their ability to strike up conversations with others more easily if they had something in common (the course, the topic, the out-of-class experience) to get them started (Finley, 2009, p. 11). Another result related to well-being that echoes the comments about alcohol use was "the positive development of social relationships. Students' connections with peers and faculty were clearly a defining, satisfying, and meaningful element of this [LC] experience" (Finley, 2009, p. 17). The research documented outcomes that were sustained beyond the first year and it controlled for selection effects, two important contributions to the literature of LCs.

Faculty at Stony Brook University (SUNY) used a quasi-experimental design to examine student performance in general chemistry courses (Hanson and Heller, 2009). Students were not randomly assigned to the courses, but the only statistically difference among the three groups was their achievement in math; one group was taking calculus and two groups were taking precalculus. Of the two groups taking precalculus, one group took their courses in an LC comprised of chemistry, precalculus, writing, and a four-credit integrative seminar, with the instructor also being the academic advisor for the LC students. Student success was measured by achievement in weekly recitation sections, weekly quizzes, course exams, and overall course grade. Across all measures, the students in the LC performed as well as or better than the students in the calculus group, and far better than the students in the other precalculus group. The authors concluded that "four principal factors can be identified for the success of students in a learning community: peer support, peer assessment, group confidence, and the learning environment" (Hanson and Heller, 2009, p. 23).

Although some research focuses on the outcomes related to different types of courses offered in LCs, other studies examine impacts on different types of students. Huerta and Bray (2008) studied LCs for first-year students at a designated Title V Hispanic-Serving Institution, looking specifically for pedagogical components of the LCs that were particularly beneficial (if they were beneficial at all) to students. They found that collaborative learning strategies were the most beneficial classroom experience for all students and that Latino students were more likely to report experiencing collaborative learning than non-Hispanic whites. The presence of collaborative learning in LCs predicted higher GPAs for students, and was associated with retention rates that were similar for Latino and non-Hispanic whites.

The results reported by Huerta and Bray (2008) were reinforced by the results of a large-scale study of LCs at four large public urban institutions that serve large numbers of underprepared students (Engstrom, 2008). Interviews were conducted with students in basic-skills LCs, and a portion of the interviews was directed toward faculty contributions to students' learning. The findings of the study "argue that faculty teaching practices created trusting, safe learning environments that promoted student persistence and success" (Engstrom, 2008, p. 8). One of the institutions reported that participation in LCs resulted in a 20–50 percent increase in student retention and success, sustained progress toward degree, and strong growth in academic and critical-thinking skills ("De Anza College: Learning in Communities: Do Learning Communities Work?," n.d.). Another institution reported higher retention rates for English as a second language (ESL) students in LCs compared with ESL students not in LCs (although not consistently higher) and substantially higher pass rates (24 percent higher one year, 33 percent higher another year) in a college-level English course for ESL students taking the course in an LC format (van Slyck, 2003). Faculty teaching practices that fostered these successes were active learning pedagogies, faculty collaboration and an integrative curriculum, development of college learning strategies, and student validation (Engstrom, 2008, p. 9). These types of teaching practices are consistent with earlier reports and calls for reform and are broadly applicable to students taking developmental and college-level courses—they enhance students' active engagement with a variety of learning processes. An example of "development of college learning strategies" was that faculty did not just tell students to form study groups and meet outside of class time, but faculty "took an active role in teaching [students] how to set up and facilitate these forums. … Students did not leave the class until they had their group and had set aside time to meet.… Faculty also used class time to encourage students to use tutors and other campus supports" (Engstrom, 2008, p. 15). These teaching practices conveyed the message to students that study groups, use of tutors, and other academic support services or activities were expected, integral parts of the course experience and not just extra work for students in trouble.

In an effort to harness the beneficial effects of LCs and service learning, some institutions combine the two, including service learning as a component of an LC. The merits of service learning are similar to those of LCs; "emerging research on service-learning validates a longstanding philosophy: integrating academics and community service delivers greater student leadership development, enriched learning, and improved academic performance" (Simonet, 2008, p. 1). Research at a midsized public research university showed that for first-time, first-year students, involvement in service learning as a part of a course increased their levels of academic and social integration (social integration with peers and with faculty) but showed significant increases in student retention only for first-time, first-year women over a two-year period (first-year to junior year) (Wolff and Tinney, 2006).

Results of student surveys at Wagner College have shown high levels of student satisfaction with LCs and with the experiential learning component of the First-Year Program (Barchitta and Eshelman, 2003). The fact that all students participate in LCs makes comparisons difficult, but from the first year to the third year of the Wagner Plan significant increases were seen in students' agreement or strong agreement with statements about the LCs such as active participation, feeling connected to students, opportunities to connect with faculty, and being challenged to improve reading, writing, and speaking skills. Commuter students reported significantly higher feelings of being connected to other students and to the campus. These higher levels were sustained after the third year of the program. Similarly, students showed significant increases in levels of agreement about the meaning of the experiential learning component of the LC, agreeing that the experiential learning made the classes meaningful, improved problem-solving skills, and increased understanding of civic responsibility.

Since the inception of the Wagner Plan, enrollments have increased with more geographic and ethnic diversity, more students living on campus, higher high school GPA and SAT scores, and higher retention rates. Faculty teaching load has been reduced but advising loads have increased, especially for the faculty teaching in the FYP. These successes have come with their own set of challenges, as facilities were stretched to and beyond capacity, including classrooms, residence halls, dining facilities, and parking lots. Retention rates hit a high in 2005 and have moderated since then, coinciding with facilities' constraints and then the economic recession. All of this is to suggest some of the institutional impacts of a successful LC program. Wagner students experienced increases in engagement and achievement, and the institution learned lessons about what it takes to sustain such momentum (Guarasci, 2006). See Chapter Three of this volume for an intradisciplinary example of the Wagner Plan in action.

Not all research on LCs shows positive results. A study of students in public speaking classes examined the relationships among social support, audience familiarity, and speaking anxiety, and the impact of LCs on those factors (Holler and Kinnick, 2008). Students in public speaking courses that were a part of an LC or were stand-alone courses were surveyed at the beginning and end of the semester. Although students in the LCs reported reduced anxiety at the end of the semester, students in the stand-alone courses reported greater reductions of anxiety. Students in the LCs reported a greater degree of comfort in giving a speech, and they were more likely to say that the other students were friends. They also were more likely to say that their audience (fellow students) was a source of anxiety than students in the stand-alone courses. The researchers speculated that the increased levels of social support and audience familiarity that were made possible by the LC format also contributed to the higher levels of anxiety; perhaps the students in the LCs were more concerned about impressing friends with whom they would continue to interact.

Recently, the National Center for Postsecondary Research and MDRC (formerly the Manpower Demonstration Research Corporation, a research organization that focuses on the well-being of low-income people) undertook research examining community college students in LCs. Citing community colleges as institutions serving students most in need of high-impact educational practices and other support mechanisms and noting the need for a more comprehensive experimental-design research study of LCs, the researchers worked with faculty at Kingsborough Community College, and currently are in the midst of a larger study involving six community colleges, the "Learning Communities Demonstration" (Visher, Wathington, Richburg-Hayes, and Schneider, 2008).

At Kingsborough, students in their first semester were placed randomly into an LC linking three courses and providing enhanced counseling and tutoring (the experimental group) or into the same courses that were not linked (the control group). Results after two years showed that students in the experimental group felt more integrated and engaged in the college, earned more credits during their first semester, and were more likely to take and pass the required English skills assessment test (Scrivener and others, 2008). Although students in the experimental group persisted at slightly higher rates than students in the control group, the difference was not statistically significant until the end of the fourth semester (three semesters after the end of the LC) (Scrivener and others, 2008, p. 61). This result emphasizes the need for assessment beyond the initial intervention, as it suggests that LCs (and other high-impact educational practices) may have an impact that accumulates over time or that takes time to become apparent.

The Learning Communities Demonstration builds upon the research and practice at Kingsborough Community College, studying six models of LCs at six community colleges (Kingsborough is one of the six, continuing the work there), and looking at design and operation of LCs, effects on student achievement, and comparative program costs. A report of the demonstration project notes that "student cohorts led to strong relationships among students, leading to both personal and academic support networks" (Visher, Schneider, Wathington, and Collado, 2010). Much of this report addresses issues related to implementation of LCs at these colleges and the associated challenges of "scaling up" from pilot programs to programs that enroll large numbers of students and require significant institutional commitment in the form of faculty and staff time and other resources. The lessons learned are applicable across many different types of higher education institutions.

Conclusion

LCs have been a growing movement aimed at educational reform for decades, and evidence continues to mount documenting successes they have achieved. Students and faculty report positive outcomes as a result of enhanced engagement with each other and the integration of ideas and experiences. At an institutional level, faculty and administrators report new partnerships, new programs, and invigorated departments as a result of LC implementation and development. Professional development for faculty and administrators is essential to the sustainability of these reform efforts (Guarasci, 2006; Levine Laufgraben and Shapiro, 2004; Smith and others, 2004). The resources listed in the Appendix are excellent opportunities for professional development, as they variously connect individuals and teams with experienced LC practitioners.

References

Astin, A. *What Matters in College*. San Francisco: Jossey-Bass, 1993.

Barchitta, J., and Eshelman, A. *The Wagner Plan: Assessments and Graphs* (Internal report). Staten Island, N.Y.: Wagner College, 2003.

Barefoot, B. O. *Second National Survey of First-Year Academic Practices*. Brevard, N.C.: Policy Center on the First Year of College, 2002.

Boyer Commission on Educating Undergraduates in the Research University. *Reinventing Undergraduate Education: A Blueprint for America's Research Universities*. Stony Brook, N.Y.: State University of New York at Stony Brook, 1998.

Buch, K., and Spaulding, S. "Using Program Assessment to 'Prove and Improve' a Discipline-Based Learning Community." *Journal of Learning Communities Research*, 2008, 3(2), 35–46.

Chickering, A. W., and Gamson, Z. F. "Seven Principles for Good Practice in Undergraduate Education." *AAHE Bulletin*, March 1987. Retrieved August 10, 2012, from http://www.aahea.org/articles/sevenprinciples1987.htm.

De Anza College. "Learning in Communties: Do Learning Communities Work?" n.d. Retrieved June 30, 2011, from http://www.deanza.edu/linc/faculty/effectiveness .html.

Engstrom, C. M. "Curricular Learning Communities and Unprepared Students: How Faculty Can Provide a Foundation for Success." *The Role of the Classroom in College Student Persistence*. New Directions for Teaching and Learning, no. 115. San Francisco: Jossey-Bass, 2008. Retrieved from www.interscience.wiley.com.

Finley, A. "The First-Year Experience and Learning Communities at Dickinson: Findings from Four Years of Research" (p. 38). Carlisle, Pa.: Dickinson College, 2009.

Gabelnick, F., MacGregor, J., Matthews, R., and Smith, B. *Learning Communities: Making Connections Among Students, Faculty, and Disciplines*. San Francisco: Jossey-Bass, 1990.

Guarasci, R. "On the Challenge of Becoming the Good College." *Liberal Education*, 2006, 92(1), 14–21.

Hanson, D. M., and Heller, J. "Learning Communities as a Strategy for Success." *International Journal of Process Education*, 2009, 1(1), 19–24.

Holler, E., and Kinnick, K. "Public Speaking Anxiety in First-Year Students: Do Learning Communities Make a Difference?" *Journal of Learning Communities Research*, 2008, 3(1), 19–41.

Huerta, J., and Bray, J. "How Do Learning Communities Affect First-year Latino Students?" *Journal of Learning Communities Research*, 2008, 3(1), 1–18.

Kuh, G. D., Kinzie, J., Schuh, J. H., and Whitt, E. J. *Student Success in College: Creating Conditions That Matter*. San Francisco: Jossey-Bass, 2005.

Lenning, O. T., and Ebbers, L. H. *The Powerful Potential of Learning Communities: Improving Education for the Future.* ASHE-ERIC Higher Education Report, Vol. 26, No. 6. Washington, D.C.: Graduate School of Education and Human Development, George Washington University, 1999.

Levine Laufgraben, J., and Shapiro, N. *Sustaining and Improving Learning Communities.* San Francisco: Jossey-Bass, 2004.

National Learning Communities Directory Search. n.d. Retrieved April 1, 2011, from http://www.evergreen.edu/washcenter/Directory.asp.

NSSE Home. n.d. Retrieved June 21, 2011, from http://nsse.iub.edu/index.cfm.

Pace, C. R. *Measuring Outcomes of College: Fifty Years of Findings and Recommendations for the Future.* San Francisco: Jossey-Bass, 1979.

Price, D. V. *Learning Communities and Student Success in Postsecondary Education: A Background Paper* (pp. 1–24). New York: MDRC, 2005. Retrieved from http://www.mdrc.org/publications/418/full.pdf.

Scrivener, S., and others. *A Good Start: Two-Year Effects of a Freshman Learning Community Program at Kingsborough Community College.* New York: MDRC, 2008. Retrieved from http://www.mdrc.org/publications/473/overview.html.

Shapiro, N., and Levine, J. *Creating Learning Communities: A Practical Guide to Winning Support, Organizing for Change, and Implementing Programs.* San Francisco: Jossey-Bass, 1999.

Simonet, D. *Service-Learning and Academic Success: The Links to Retention Research.* Minneapolis: Minnesota Campus Compact, 2008. Retrieved from http://www.mncampuscompact.org/vertical/sites/%7BE34AF879-F177–472C-9EB0-D811F247058B%7D/uploads/%7B0FFFDCFD-F60E-4067-ACC3–701824101883%7D.PDF.

Smith, B. L., and MacGregor, J. "Learning Communities and the Quest for Quality." *Quality Assurance in Education,* 2009, *17*(2), 118–139.

Smith, B. L., MacGregor, J., Matthews, R. S., and Gabelnick, F. *Learning Communities: Reforming Undergraduate Education.* San Francisco: Jossey-Bass, 2004.

Taylor, K., Moore, W. S., MacGregor, J., & Lindblad, J. *Learning Community Research and Assessment: What We Know Now.* National Learning Communities Project Monograph Series. Olympia, Wash.: Washington Center for Improving the Quality of Undergraduate Education, The Evergreen State College, 2003.

Tinto, V. *Leaving College: Rethinking the Causes and Cures of Student Attrition.* Chicago: University of Chicago Press, 1987.

Tinto, V., Goodsell, A., and Russo, P. *Building Learning Communities for New College Students.* State College, Pa.: National Center on Postsecondary Teaching, Learning, and Assessment, Pennsylvania State University, 1994.

Tussman, J. *Experiment at Berkeley.* New York: Oxford University Press, 1969.

van Slyck, P. "Developmental and ESL Learning Communities at LaGuardia Community College." 2003. Retrieved from http://www.lagcc.cuny.edu/lc/overview/pdfs/devcomm.pdf.

Visher, M., Schneider, E., Wathington, H., and Collado, H. *Scaling Up Learning Communities: The Experience of Six Community Colleges.* New York: MDRC, 2010. Retrieved from http://www.mdrc.org/publications/550/overview.html.

Visher, M., Wathington, H., Richburg-Hayes, L., and Schneider, E. *The Learning Communities Demonstration: Rationale, Sites, and Research Design.* New York: MDRC, 2008. Retrieved from http://www.mdrc.org/publications/476/overview.html.

Wolff, M., and Tinney, S. "Service-Learning and College Student Success." *Academic Exchange Quarterly,* 2006, *10*(1), 57–61.

Zhao, C.-M., and Kuh, G. D. "Adding Value: Learning Communities and Student Engagement." *Research in Higher Education,* 2004, *45*(2), 115–138.

ANNE GOODSELL LOVE is associate provost for assessment at Wagner College, coordinating collegewide assessment efforts. In addition, she has been codirector of the Atlantic Center for Learning Communities, a regional leadership network dedicated to supporting colleges and universities in their development of learning communities and other learner-centered pedagogies.

NEW DIRECTIONS FOR TEACHING AND LEARNING • DOI: 10.1002/tl

2

Curriculum-based learning communities centered within a discipline can take on many forms. Through the use of specific institutional examples, this chapter examines three models requiring minimal to more complex coordination.

Curriculum-Based Learning Communities Centered Within a Discipline

Mark C. Zrull, Courtney A. Rocheleau, M. Corinne Smith, Shawn M. Bergman

This chapter focuses on curriculum-based learning communities (LCs). In these LCs, manipulation of the curriculum is intentional and often innovative (Lenning and Ebbers, 1999), with the overarching goals of developing meaningful connections among students, between students and faculty, and between students and their coursework (see Gabelnick and others, 1990). The original LC experiments by Meiklejohn and Tussman (highlighted in Chapter One) represent forms of curriculum-based LCs in which the curriculum of all or most of a group of students was coordinated. This approach is only one of many forms for curriculum-based LCs. In fact, the variety of curriculum-based models reflect the general strength of LCs to be flexible and to meet specific demands of various colleges and universities and the different student groups within those institutions (MacGregor and Smith, 2005). One "flexibility" is to center an LC within a particular discipline, such as psychology, as featured in this book.

However, despite these variations, a commonality across all curriculum-based LC models is having students coenrolled in two or more courses. Curriculum-based LCs may offer experiences during the first year alone, include opportunities for involvement over multiple years or begin in the sophomore, junior, or senior year. In the remainder of the chapter, we present examples of three models of curriculum-based LCs, a more detailed description of a specific discipline-centered curriculum-based LC

NEW DIRECTIONS FOR TEACHING AND LEARNING, no. 132, Winter 2012 © Wiley Periodicals, Inc.
Published online in Wiley Online Library (wileyonlinelibrary.com) • DOI: 10.1002/tl.20033

at Appalachian State University, and conclude with some advantages and disadvantages of curriculum-based LCs centered in a discipline.

Models of Discipline-Centered Curriculum-Based LCs

Since the earliest incarnations, various curriculum-based LC models have been proposed (Gabelnick and others, 1990; Lenning and Ebbers, 1999). Current practices include three general models from which specific curriculum-based LCs emerge: embedded cohort, multiple linked courses, and coordinated studies (Barron and others, 2010; MacGregor and Smith, 2005). Searches of two excellent LC databases at the Learning Communities National Resource Center sponsored by Evergreen State College (http://www.evergreen.edu/washcenter/project.asp?pid=73) and at the Residential Learning Communities International Clearinghouse at Bowling Green State University (http://pcc.bgsu.edu/rlcch/submissions/) reveal that all three general models of discipline-centered, curriculum-based LCs can be found across various colleges and universities.

Embedded Cohort Model. The embedded cohort model is the easiest way to implement a curriculum-based LC within a discipline in that it does not require extensive coordination or the use of additional curricular resources. The model makes use of existing course sections and places a group of LC students within one or more courses (Barron and others, 2010; MacGregor and Smith, 2005). In this model disciplinary courses are not specific to the LC, and LC students are enrolled in courses with non-LC students. This embedding of students also means that there need not be an explicit effort to coordinate material across courses used by the cohort of LC students. However, to provide an opportunity for LC members to make better connections among themselves, with faculty, and with the college or university as a community, students can be enrolled in an additional seminar taught only to LC members.

A discipline-centered example of an embedded cohort curricular LC can be found at the University of North Carolina Charlotte. In this LC, first-year students who indicate psychology as a potential major are targeted. Students must submit an additional application to be considered, and once selected are enrolled as a cohort within existing sections of General Psychology and General Psychology lab. In addition, smaller, subcohorts of LC students are coenrolled in a general education course. However, to enhance students' connections with each other and the discipline of psychology, students are enrolled in a freshman seminar open only to psychology LC students. The curriculum of the freshman seminar includes career and professional development activities along with a service-learning component to obtain a psychology-related practitioner experience in the community (Buch and Barron, 2011). Additional information about the LC and the impact it is having on students can be found in a variety of sources (for

example, Buch and Barron, 2011) or on-line (http://www.psych.uncc.edu
/PLC.htm).

First-year, discipline-centered curricular LCs can also reflect a starting
point for related disciplines rather than a single major. For example, at the
University of Saskatchewan a series of curricular LCs are available for students (http://www.usask.ca/ulc/lc/about). The common goals across the
LCs are "connectedness and directedness" in both the academic program
and career guidance. To achieve these goals, the Saskatchewan LCs draw a
pair of courses from different but connected disciplines, include a supporting course common to the disciplines, and embed a cohort of LC students
in the three courses. For example, the Social Science LC places a cohort
into the same sections of introductory psychology and sociology courses as
well as an English course, whereas the Science and Research LC embeds a
cohort in initial biology and chemistry courses as well as an English course.

Linked Multiple Courses Model. The linked multiple courses curricular LC model is more difficult to implement in a discipline than the
embedded cohorts model in that two or more courses or sections of courses
are made available only to LC members (Barron and others, 2010;
Gabelnick and others, 1990). In this model, connections and community
are established in courses enrolling only LC members, which requires
resources available only to LC students. However, a benefit of this model is
that it allows for implicit or explicit integration of material across courses
as well as activities outside the classroom.

A discipline-centered example of a linked multiple courses curricular
LC can be found at James Madison University. Once again, first-year students who have declared psychology as a major are targeted. During the fall
semester, LC students enroll in special sections of courses taught exclusively to LC members: Orientation to Psychology and the Major and Psychological Research Methods and Data Analysis I. The community
members then take Psychological Research Methods and Data Analysis II as
a group during the spring term. Through the linked courses and additional
out-of-class experiences, students connect with the discipline, in this case
psychology, and with each other as a community. For more information see
Barron and others (2010) and Buch and Barron (2011) as well as http://
www.jmu.edu/orl/involved/psychology.htm.

Another excellent example of a linked multiple courses model for
seniors in their discipline occurs at Wagner College and is the focus of
Chapter Three.

Coordinated Studies Model. Perhaps the most difficult discipline-
centered, curriculum-based LC model to implement is a coordinated studies model. In coordinated studies models, faculty and students are essentially full-time members of the community. That is, a limited number of
faculty teach courses almost exclusively or only in the LC program with the
LC students primarily taking only LC courses in a particular term or across
terms. This arrangement allows for greater integration of material across

courses as only a limited number of, and often the same, faculty are teaching multiple LC courses in a given term. Similarly, communication among the faculty is fostered as they primarily have the same LC students in all or most of their classes (Barron and others, 2010; Lenning and Ebbers, 1999).

To center such an arrangement within a discipline is rather difficult as faculty, space, and scheduling time are devoted exclusively to the coordinated studies LC. However, this approach can allow the most flexibility in developing an LC curriculum (see MacGregor and Smith, 2005) because following a traditional semester schedule is not required and boundaries between courses can be easily blurred (Barron and others, 2010). In fact, some coordinated studies LCs have no specific courses; rather, a variety of topics are approached using various teaching methods including seminars, lectures, individual study, field studies, and laboratories. Although more coordinated studies curriculum-based LC models are interdisciplinary than are centered in a discipline, examples of the coordinated studies model centered within psychology are offered at Evergreen State College as well as Skagit State College and George Mason University.

For example, Evergreen State has a reputation for developing innovative and team-taught academic programs. The Clinical Psychology: The Scientist Practitioner Model LC at Evergreen is a yearlong, sixteen-credit-hour per term coordinated studies LC for sophomores through seniors. During the first quarter, students study history and systems of psychology as well as quantitative and qualitative research methods. In the subsequent two quarters, students engage in a fifteen-hour per week, regionally based internship as well as studying personality and psychopathology and then forms of psychotherapy. Each quarter, topical areas are approached in classroom seminars, and individual and group research projects that culminate with presentations made to the entire LC.

The Consciousness LC at Evergreen is a single-quarter program for freshmen through seniors that approaches the topic of consciousness from neuroscience, psychological, mindfulness, and spiritual perspectives. Initially, LC members work together to create the program syllabus, and then the community engages in learning through seminars, individual research, group work, and presentations. For more information about the vast array of LCs at Evergreen State, see the catalog at http://www.evergreen.edu/catalog.

We hope readers appreciate that the three major models of curriculum-based LCs outlined in this chapter offer much room for flexibility. Beyond making curricular connections, many of these initiatives are combined with having students living in the same residence hall to create an integrated living–learning community. In fact, a number of the LCs showcased here incorporate a residential component (for more information about creating residential-based LCs, see Chapter Four). Further, the formal academic components of curriculum-based LCs are often more apparent than the informal extracurricular components of these programs. However, these out-of-class activities are at least as important as traditional class activities in meeting curriculum-based LC goals. A glimpse into possibilities for customization and extracurricular components can be illustrated by taking an in-depth look at one curriculum-based LC program, the Brain Matters LC at Appalachian State University.

Brain Matters: A Discipline-Centered, Embedded Cohort Curriculum-Based LC

The Brain Matters LC at Appalachian is a combined curricular–residential-based LC focused on psychology and the behavioral sciences. Brain Matters was created in fall 2010 to enhance students' first-year experience and has served approximately forty freshmen members during each of its first two years. Brain Matters students live together in a residence hall, take psychology-related courses together, and participate in a number of events and activities outside the classroom that serve to build community and connect students to the curricular focus of the LC.

Brain Matters was first conceptualized by a senior member of the psychology faculty and a staff member in university housing. These individuals, with an additional three departmental faculty, comprise the Brain Matters leadership team. Together, the leadership team developed and refined a mission, vision, and values statement to guide the LC (http://housing.appstate.edu/pagesmith/123; see also Rocheleau and others, 2011) and determined its basic structure (for example, target number of students, LC-associated coursework). The leadership team also includes two students, the resident assistant (RA) and graduate resident director (RD) of the residence hall where the LC is housed. This distribution of responsibility for the LC equally across the housing and disciplinary members of the leadership team is one aspect of Brain Matters that differs from many models of residential curriculum-based LCs. Often, leadership of a residential curriculum-based LC reflects one group's interests to a greater degree, with the other serving in an advisory, or otherwise ancillary, capacity. In the case of Brain Matters, the students, faculty, and housing staff work together to shape the LC's goals and activities (Rocheleau and others, 2011).

A number of factors led to the decision to use an embedded cohort model for Brain Matters. First, this model had been successfully implemented at Appalachian in other disciplines and interest areas. Second, the embedded cohort model allowed us to include a more diverse cross-section of students by recruiting first-year students intending to major in psychology as well as those with only an interest in psychology. Many LC members plan to major in related disciplines (for example, premedical, prelaw, sociology, education) or have informal interests in behavioral science. Because the embedded cohort model requires students to take only a handful of courses together, they can participate in the LC even if they do not plan to major in psychology. This flexibility allows Brain Matters to attract a diverse group of students, including targeting underserved and underrepresented populations in psychology. For example, although there is a trend toward the "feminization" of psychology (Littleford and others, 2010), Brain Matters includes equal numbers of men and women. We have found that having a diverse community membership (in terms of intended major and traditional demographic characteristics) has provided for a richer experience by bringing together individuals with different skills, worldviews, and experiences. Finally, the embedded cohort model requires the fewest dedicated resources from the disciplinary department. In the case of Brain Matters, these included a block of seats reserved for LC members in extant classes and one or two sections of a first-year seminar dedicated to LC students.

Students take one of two dedicated first-year seminars, which focus on interdisciplinary topics that have strong ties to psychology, the brain, and behavioral sciences. The Brain: A User's Guide has a central theme of neuroanatomy and neurophysiology as these relate to behavior and a wide variety of phenomena. Black Cats, Placebos, & Lotteries focuses on the critical evaluation of empirical evidence in making decisions, rather than relying on intuition and superstition. LC members also enroll as small groups within larger courses made up of non-LC students. In the first semester, Brain Matters students may coenroll in a larger section of an introductory psychology course alongside non-LC students. In the second semester, Brain Matters students have the opportunity to take part as embedded cohorts in intermediate-level courses offered in the major. As the registration period for the second semester approaches, the first-year seminar instructors invite students to identify which of the five intermediate-level courses in psychology they would be interested in taking the following term. Based on sufficient interest, the department blocks off seats for LC students. This ensures that LC students will be able to register in these courses despite the late registration dates associated with their freshman status. Although the majority of students in these courses are not LC members, the reserved seats for LC students in one section of each course allows for the embedded cohorts. Because these courses are required for majors in related departments, even LC members who do not intend to major in psychology can benefit from this opportunity.

Although these course experiences are important in achieving the mission and goals of Brain Matters, extracurricular programming and informal interactions among LC members are integral to the LC. These include interactions among students and between students and LC faculty. Although such interactions may appear at first blush to be less valuable because they are less structured, we have found these to be invaluable in building a sense of community and allowing for less hierarchical and more fluid roles of all LC members, providing a richer experience for all community members (including faculty, staff, and students). In addition to the traditional course experiences, the Brain Matters leadership team provides psychology-related programming for LC members monthly throughout the academic year. These programs are one-time events focusing on a specific content area within the behavioral sciences and designed to reflect diverse areas within the discipline. Because Brain Matters is a residential LC, the students also have regular programming provided by RAs.

Examples of additional LC programming included a faculty member providing a tour of the animal research laboratory and discussing his research in behavioral neuroscience. Another program featured a panel of faculty who answered questions about romantic relationships based on research on intimate relationships. Another featured a cognitive psychology faculty member discussing empirically supported study strategies students could use for long-term retention of course material. Finally, some programs are social events with faculty and students making and sharing a meal while engaged in informal and impromptu discussions about psychology, behavioral science, and other things important to students. These programs help to expose students to the science and application of psychology in an informal setting and include a social component, intended to reinforce the community development within the LC as well as foster relationships among Brain Matters students and faculty.

To assess the success of the LC, the Brain Matters leadership team developed a plan to determine the extent to which the LC achieved the goals and outcomes outlined in the mission and vision statements. This plan includes quantitative (for example, examining first-year grade point average [GPA] and retention, course evaluations for the first-year seminar course, numerical ratings of community members' satisfaction) and qualitative elements (for example, comments from focus groups at the end of the fall semester, surveys of LC students, self-assessment by leadership team at the end of the spring semester). Input about the performance of the LC was sought from all stakeholders, including faculty, housing staff, and students. Because Brain Matters is only in its second year, conclusions regarding the LC's success should be considered preliminary at this point. Available data suggest that outcomes for Brain Matters' first year were similar to outcomes of other residential LCs at Appalachian, including LC students achieving higher GPAs than non-LC students and increased retention from the first semester to second semester and from the first year to the second year. In addition, and as we hoped, students and faculty involved in the LC report high degrees of satisfaction with their experience.

Benefits of Curriculum-Based LCs and Lessons Learned

Like all LCs, curriculum-based LCs began and continue because the involved faculty and student affairs professionals believe the advantages outweigh any disadvantages of implementing and maintaining these programs. Although it is difficult to provide a concise overview of advantages of curriculum-based LCs given the variety and combination of models, most reviews suggest that outcomes (including academic success and academic and social student engagement) are similar for undergraduate members of all LCs with a curricular component. For example, Brownell and Swaner (2010) reviewed studies examining outcomes for LCs with clear curricular connections and found that after controlling for demographics and precollege background, academic achievement and persistence toward academic goals are enhanced for LC students. Barron and others (2010) reported similar achievement trends for embedded cohort and linked multiple course models of psychology-centered, curriculum-based LCs. Specifically, LC students had higher major GPAs and overall GPAs and made more progress toward completing psychology major requirements than matched groups of non-LC students. Stassen (2003) suggested that although the more structured models, such as coordinated studies curriculum-based LCs, achieve the greatest success on outcomes measures, membership in any curriculum-based LC has a positive impact on academic success (that is, GPA and persistence).

Beyond producing advantages in academic achievement and retention, curricular LCs affect academic and social engagement. Among those outcomes reported for LC members in comparison to students not in LCs include greater classroom engagement and taking more intellectual risks (Brownell and Swaner, 2010), increased student–faculty interaction both in the classroom and during out-of-class experiences (Inkelas and Weisman, 2003), and promoting greater appreciation for pursuing diverse points of view (Cross, 1998). The results of the National Study of Living Learning Programs (Brower and Inkelas, 2010) also indicated LCs that had a curricular connection (that is, "course-related faculty interaction," p. 41) predicted student gains in critical thinking, applying knowledge, and successful transition to college academics.

Although the outcomes of primary interest rightly center on students' academic performance and development, it is interesting to note that development and maintenance of curricular LCs can lead to positive connections between academic affairs and student affairs as well as within an academic department (MacGregor and Smith, 2005). At Appalachian, we have noticed that curriculum-based LCs help student affairs staff build connections with an entire department rather than just with individuals across multiple departments.

Further, student members of a discipline-centered curriculum-based LC know what they are getting. Students know that when they sign up for this type of LC, they are going to be focusing on a particular discipline as the foundation of their LC mission, programming, and interactions. Thus, students are less likely to be disappointed in their LC choice and may actually value the LC experience more, knowing that their discipline-centered LC is tied to a potential major and future career.

Of course, implementing and developing curriculum-based LCs is not without its shortcomings. Students in a discipline-centered curriculum-based LC may receive something of a mixed message regarding the breadth and interdisciplinarity of general education, something that is important and beneficial in college and often championed by curriculum-based LCs (see Lenning and Ebbers, 1999; MacGregor and Smith, 2005). Similarly, it is possible that a more narrow scholarly approach than fostered by a liberal, general education too early in a student's undergraduate career might inadvertently reduce diversity in thought or attitude (see Brownell and Swaner, 2010). However, as an appreciation of interdisciplinarity and diversity in thinking are typically valued goals of LCs (Brower and Inkelas, 2010; Inkelas and Wiseman, 2003), this risk of thought or attitude reduction can be minimized if the curriculum-based LC leaders are mindful of this potential challenge and capitalize on opportunities for highlighting areas of interdisciplinarity and diverse thinking. Thus, a well-designed curriculum-based LC centered on a discipline can make connections between concepts and disciplines and avoid the potential disciplinary tunnel vision of a poorly designed discipline-centered curriculum-based LC.

Finally, involvement in any high-impact program, such as a discipline-centered curriculum-based LC, by faculty or student affairs staff often requires effort and commitment usually beyond standard teaching, scholarship, and service expectations. At Appalachian, Brain Matters leadership team members have learned a few lessons that seem important and help keep rewards outweighing any extra work. First, your initial meeting with LC students is critical and needs to allow for interaction among LC students and all leadership team members including the faculty. At your initial meeting, take the time to ask students why they picked this particular LC and what they hope to gain. Second, do not let the LC become insular. Extracurricular programming for Brain Matters often involves non-LC faculty; however, one or more faculty from the LC leadership team attend these events and friends of Brain Matters students who want to attend events are not excluded. This structure supports more formal and informal integration among LC members as well as with other non-LC faculty and students from our department, which supports and reinforces the benefits of the LC's diverse nature. Third, as the year progresses, invite a student to become a member of the LC leadership team. During the second semester, the Brain Matters leadership team includes a student member who attends planning meetings, which allows better anticipation of student interests and needs. Finally, all stakeholders in an LC need to be flexible. For Brain Matters, we discovered that communities can vary greatly and that the nature of programming and events needs to be adaptable to the nature of a particular community.

Conclusion

Certainly, the three models of discipline-centered, curriculum-based LCs described in this chapter are not exhaustive; however, they do provide an

NEW DIRECTIONS FOR TEACHING AND LEARNING • DOI: 10.1002/tl

overview and examples of ways in which various types of curriculum-based LCs have been successfully implemented at a variety of institutions within a single discipline. Although the evidence for the efficacy of specific curriculum-based LCs is difficult to obtain, systematic and anecdotal evidence suggests that curriculum-based LCs, in general as well as in specific disciplines, have a positive impact on a variety of academic and social outcomes for the students who participate in them. Finally, the notion of centering a curriculum-based LC in a discipline may not be so contrary to the interdisciplinarity often championed as a hallmark of LCs as it seems. Disciplinary LCs promote student learning and engagement in varied contexts supporting connections to peers, faculty, and the academic experience.

References

Barron, K. E., Buch, K. K., Andre, J. T., and Spaulding, S. "Learning Communities as an Innovative Beginning to the Psychology Major. A Tale of Two Campuses." In D. S. Dunn, B. C. Beins, M. A. McCarthy, and G. W. Hill IV (eds.), *Best Practices for Teaching Beginnings and Endings in the Psychology Major: Research, Cases, and Recommendations.* New York: Oxford University Press, 2010.

Brower, A. H., and Inkelas, K. K. "Living Learning Programs: One High-Impact Educational Practice We Know a Lot About." *Liberal Education,* 2010, 96(2), 36–43.

Brownell, J. E., and Swaner, L. E. "Chapter 2: Learning Communities." In *Five High-Impact Practices: Research on Learning Outcomes, Completion, and Quality.* Washington, D.C.: Association of American Colleges & Universities, 2010.

Buch, K., and Barron, K. E. "Increasing Student Engagement through Curricular-Based Learning Communities." In R. L. Miller, and others (eds.), *Promoting Student Engagement. Vol. 1: Programs, Techniques and Opportunities.* Washington, D.C.: Society for Teaching Psychology, 2011. Retrieved May 31, 2011, from http://teachpsych.org /resources/e-books/pse2011/vol1/.

Cross, K.P. "Why Learning Communities? Why Now?" *About Campus,* 1998, 3(3), 4–11.

Gabelnick, F., MacGregor, J., Matthews, R. S., and Smith, B. L. *Learning Communities: Creating Connections Among Students, Faculty, and Disciplines.* New Directions for Teaching and Learning, no. 41. San Francisco: Jossey-Bass, 1990.

Inkelas, K. K., and Weisman, J. L. "Different by Design: An Examination of Student Outcomes Among Participants in Three Types of Living-Learning Programs." *Journal of College Student Development,* 2003, 44(3), 335–368.

Lenning, O. T., and Ebbers, L. H. *The Powerful Potential of Learning Communities: Improving Education for the Future.* ASHE-ERIC Higher Education Report, Vol. 26, No. 6. Washington, D.C.: George Washington University, 1999.

Littleford, L. N., and others. "Psychology Students Today and Tomorrow." In D. F. Halpern (ed.), *Undergraduate Education in Psychology: A Blueprint for the Future of the Discipline.* Washington, D.C.: American Psychological Association, 2010.

MacGregor, J., and Smith, B. L. "Where Are Learning Communities Now? National Leaders Take Stock." *About Campus,* 2005, 10(2), 2–8.

Rocheleau, C. A., Smith, M. C., Bergman, S., and Zrull, M. C. "Residential Learning Communities in Psychology: How to Get Started." In R. L. Miller, and others (eds.), *Promoting Student Engagement. Vol. 1: Programs, Techniques and Opportunities.* Washington, D.C.: Society for Teaching Psychology, 2011. Retrieved May 31, 2011, from http://teachpsych.org/resources/e-books/pse2011/vol1/.

Stassen, M.L.A. "Student Outcomes: The Impact of Varying Living-Learning Community Models." *Research in Higher Education,* 2003, 44(5), 581–613.

MARK C. ZRULL is a professor in the Department of Psychology at Appalachian State University.

COURTNEY A. ROCHELEAU is an assistant professor in the Department of Psychology at Appalachian State University.

M. CORINNE SMITH is a residence life and learning communities coordinator in University Housing at Appalachian State University.

SHAWN M. BERGMAN is an assistant professor in the Department of Psychology at Appalachian State University.

NEW DIRECTIONS FOR TEACHING AND LEARNING • DOI: 10.1002/tl

3

This chapter describes the senior learning community in psychology at Wagner College, which is an example of a discipline-specific curriculum-based learning community (LC). This LC acts both as a capstone to the undergraduate experience and as a transition for students from college to career. We describe the components of the LC, their development, our attempts to integrate them, and how they might be applied in other intradisciplinary LCs.

Transitioning Students Out of College: The Senior LC in Psychology at Wagner College

Laurence J. Nolan, Steve M. Jenkins

At Wagner College, students are required to participate in a series of three curriculum-based learning communities (C-BLCs) as the core of the undergraduate curriculum known as the Wagner Plan for the Practical Liberal Arts. In this curriculum, we attempt to bring together a liberal arts education and practical application by taking advantage of our geographic location in New York City (Wagner College, 2011a). Learning communities (LCs) are essential to this mission (see the introductory chapter of this volume for a description of the role of the LC in the Wagner Plan). The first two LCs are interdisciplinary in scope and traditionally designed in that they are typically composed of two separate linked courses (of the type described by Lenning and Ebbers, 1999, and by Zrull, Rocheleau, Smith, and Bergman in Chapter Two). All first-year students are enrolled in an LC composed of two courses linked around a theme. For example, the first author of this chapter taught (for six years) an introductory psychology course paired with an introductory biology course in an LC titled Sense & Nonsense in Science. In it, students explored how to separate real science from pseudoscience in health and science research. The second author is in his sixth year of teaching an LC titled Mind, Body & Culture, which explores questions of culture, evolution, and health through a pairing of introductory courses in anthropology and psychology. All first-year LCs include a third course (reflective tutorial) that emphasizes intensive writing

New Directions for Teaching and Learning, no. 132, Winter 2012 © Wiley Periodicals, Inc.
Published online in Wiley Online Library (wileyonlinelibrary.com) • DOI: 10.1002/tl.20034

and is linked to thirty hours of experiential learning in the city. In the second or third year, all students enroll in an intermediate learning community (ILC) that emphasizes curricular integration (Guarasci, 2006). For example, the first author of this chapter coteaches an ILC on eating behavior, food, and cuisine with a member of the history department. Research from the two disciplines is used to answer questions regarding why we eat what we eat (and why we eat it this way and not another), and how that might be influenced by psychological, physiological, historical, and public policy factors. In all ILCs, the courses culminate in a significant interdisciplinary written project. Unlike the first semester LC, many students in the ILC have begun their specialized major course of study. The ILC brings them back to take an interdisciplinary approach to specific questions.

The Senior Program at Wagner has at its core the senior LC (SLC), which encourages students to examine how their field of study is practiced in the "real world." Unlike the previous LCs, it is intradisciplinary and takes place within the student's major department. Like the other LCs at Wagner, the SLC follows a linked course format. Specifically, the SLC is composed of a capstone course, which is a cumulative content course that serves to reintegrate the major (Guarasci, 2006), and a reflective tutorial (RFT), which is designed to provide an opportunity for in-class reflection on the links between the course content, field experience (a 100-hour practicum meant to provide experience in how the discipline is practiced in a profession), and professional practice (Wagner College, 2011a). Although the LC takes on the appearance of two linked courses, it actually contains three components: the capstone course, the RFT, and the field experience. Senior capstone courses (and senior seminars) are fairly common, but they tend to focus on developing critical thinking and communication skills separately from programs that prepare students for careers (Hensheid, 2008). At Wagner, these are brought together in the SLC. Because of the variety of departments involved, several SLC models have been adopted. Although most use the linked course model described earlier and offer the SLC annually, some departments (for example, biological sciences) use a sequence of courses in the final year (RFT follows a content area capstone course) whereas others, with small majors (for example, art), allow junior students to enroll in an SLC offered in alternate years (Wagner College, 2011a). In psychology, the SLC Psychology: Then and Now is designed to help students explore the philosophical and historical foundations of psychology and examine how they are related to current psychological research, theory, and practice (Wagner College, 2011b). Both the capstone and the RFT meet twice each week, usually on the same days of the week. Participation in the SLC is required for all students who are psychology majors. Although on some campuses graduating seniors may be more difficult to define than the entering class is (Hensheid, 2008), our students are traditional, full-time students, and most are seniors preparing for

NEW DIRECTIONS FOR TEACHING AND LEARNING • DOI: 10.1002/tl

graduation four years after beginning their education at Wagner. Next, we describe the components of the LC, the development of these components, and our attempts to integrate them. This discussion is informed by assessments performed annually by the psychology department; a description of that process will follow.

The Capstone Course

The capstone course is a fairly traditional content course on the history of psychology and normally enrolls about twenty-five students. The course is taught in a discussion format and students are assigned readings from a textbook and primary sources written by influential figures in and contemporary scholars of the history of psychology. When the LC was created, this course was the logical choice for the capstone given that it had been the senior-level required course for the major prior to implementation of learning communities at Wagner College. It was therefore designed as a cumulative experience for students who had already developed a certain level of sophistication in the discipline during their previous three years of study. Because a theme of the course is the relevance of the history of ideas in psychology to contemporary professional psychology, it was also possible to link it to a field experience in the RFT. The course syllabus explicitly states that a major goal is to explore the development of ideas in psychology and how they have framed contemporary debate. In addition to discussions of the historical origins of contemporary issues in experimental psychology, there are comparable discussions regarding professional and applied psychology relevant to the RFT practicum. Some of the primary sources directly challenge students' views of what psychology is and the value of its contributions. One reading challenges students to think about what the various areas of psychology have in common and whether psychology itself is a unified single field. Another questions whether neuroscience research has told us anything practical about how the brain works and whether psychotherapy or pharmacotherapy offers any benefits for consumers.

The Reflective Tutorial

The RFT was developed in response to the implementation of the Wagner Plan. Prior to its creation, field placements were available, but students enrolled in them independently and met individually with their faculty advisor rather than together for class discussion or reflection. In the RFT, students are asked to link their classroom-based education experiences to their field experience and engage in a reflective process regarding decisions made in these experiences. Having students engaged in field work meet together in a group to discuss their experiences, instead of alone with a supervising faculty member, may offer significant advantages such as peer support and learning about field experiences different from their own (see Bay, 2006, for a description of its use with senior English majors). Although it is fairly simple to create objectives that reflect the stated goals and spirit of the Wagner Plan, it is quite another thing to turn these objectives into practice. As we discuss, over the last five years, revisions to the course have attempted to more fully engage students in their learning, while at the same time meet the goals of the department and the college, keeping in mind the needs of our seniors for their life endeavors after graduation.

The RFT Field Placement. One of the requirements of the Senior RFT is that students must complete a 100-hour field placement. It is the role of the professor to help students obtain field placements that best fit their interests and goals and to supervise these placements. As students are also busy with other courses during the semester, they usually need the entire semester to complete these hours (usually one day per week). Hence, it is in their best interest to begin the semester with a placement already secured. To make sure that students are appropriately prepared, a mandatory meeting with students occurs at the end of the prior semester to facilitate this process. Topics discussed during this meeting include field placements and how to go about researching a placement site, how to contact a placement site, phone and e-mail etiquette, as well as working with the college's Center for Academic and Career Development office to put together vitae and cover letters and learn the basics of interviewing. Students acquire the tools they need to secure a placement, but the placement is never directly set up for them. Students are informed that networking and interviewing are highly valuable skills that they need to practice and develop.

The interests and career goals of psychology majors are extremely diverse, and students are challenged to find a placement site that will provide them with the most valuable experience. Each semester students are required to complete a succinct review of their placement that includes contact information, a summary of duties performed, and strengths and weaknesses of the placement. This ongoing compilation of summaries serves as a valuable resource for future students in the psychology RFT who are looking for a specific type of placement. Students can review this catalog to see if they find a potential match for their interests. Most students do find a placement from this catalog; however, this does not work for every student, and other options for obtaining a unique placement are discussed. For example, one recent student had a strong interest in mentoring children of color. After some research, she found out that there was a center that serves African immigrants to New York a few miles from campus. The agency staff were more than happy to have her volunteer there, working with boys and girls in their after-school program. Another student wanted to gain some practical experience in physiological psychology and obtained a placement at the traumatic brain injury unit of a local hospital.

Students with other interests have completed their field placements in marketing firms, elementary schools that specialize in children with developmental disorders, outpatient and inpatient psychiatric facilities, and many more. Options for students, especially in a large metropolitan area, are almost unlimited. However, prior to beginning a placement at a new agency, students must submit a proposal to the RFT professor that includes a description of the placement, duties that will be performed, and how the placement will enhance their knowledge of a psychologically related field. Most proposals are accepted, but this process requires students to think critically about their placement site before they begin.

RFT Reading Assignments. One particular challenge for the senior RFT is that, unlike many survey courses, there are no formal textbooks to fall back on for guidance. The professor is charged with finding literature appropriate for the course that will facilitate learning in the placement and promote active reflection. When the course was first developed, the bulk of the course readings pertained to careers in psychology and included discussion of textbooks and primary literature on various careers in the field. In addition, students were required to pair with each other to compile research on a particular career and present their findings to the class. Although this course strategy worked well in exposing students to a wide range of opportunities potentially available to them, it was lacking in a few areas. First, it was often difficult for some students to connect the readings to their placements. A student working with individuals in a traumatic brain injury unit would have difficulty reflecting on how a career in industrial–organizational psychology was related to his or her placement. Second, some of the readings were not adequately linked to historical concepts in psychology, the other course in the LC.

In revising the course, it was necessary to find a way to broaden the reading material so that students in various placements could aptly reflect on how they were using psychological principles in the work they were doing at their placement sites. In addition, the readings needed to more closely tie in the current psychological research, theory, and practice to the historical foundations of psychology. However, a primary goal of the RFT is to provide a space for students to reflect on their future career choices, so any revisions had to maintain that component.

The first change made to the readings was to drop the two required texts on careers in psychology, and simply recommend them to students. They were replaced with readings of primary literature that focused on how the historical concepts that students were learning in the capstone course remain applicable today in the very work that students were doing in their placements. Articles such as "Does Psychology Make a Significant Difference in Our Lives?" by Phillip Zimbardo (2004) trace many of the accomplishments made by early psychologists that affect our lives today. Other examples are articles that discuss replications of classic social psychology studies and how the results of these studies affect the field today. Each week students are required to turn in an extensive reflection of how that week's reading is related to previous courses, research studies, controversial issues in psychology, current events, and life experiences. These broader readings and detailed instruction on the reflection process has led to greater student interest and more productive class discussion.

RFT Career Discussion. According to the U.S. Bureau of Labor Statistics, the average U.S. worker changes jobs frequently (five times in the first eight years of a career) (Light, 2005). Hence, it is prudent for students to be exposed to options that would be open to them with a psychology degree. To pique student interest, a few readings and class discussion on the importance of work and career to psychological health are offered. Next, each student is required to research the details of a career that he or she was considering moving into after college. Finally, students begin the process of "learning by doing," a regularly stated goal of the Wagner Plan. To gain a more complete picture of what a job is like, career counselors often suggest that individuals interview people who are actually working in that particular job. After deciding as a class on the most important questions to ask, students are required to seek out a person currently working in his or her ideal job and give a presentation on similarities and differences between what the research states and the reality of a particular career according to their interviewee. With presentations that reflect the real-life experiences of individuals performing the daily tasks in a particular career, student interest and class discussions have become significantly richer.

In their review of the literature on the transition from college to career, Wendlandt and Rochlen (2008) report that students experience significant difficulty when they move from school to work and that a considerable amount of this is caused by a lack of understanding of work culture, inexperience working with others (especially those of different ages), and unrealistic expectations about their role as an employee. Although it is tempting to think of graduating students as "finishing," Chickering and Schlossberg (1998) encourage a lifespan development approach when discussing the changes associated with the college to career transition. It is possible for colleges to implement programs to reduce these difficulties, because socialization for work starts in college as students begin to anticipate entry into a career and begin gathering information and determining what types of organizations appeal to them (Wendlandt and Rochlen, 2008). Requiring students to interact with organizations through fieldwork experiences and internships and providing an active learning environment where students are asked to apply theoretical knowledge to genuine problems and real-life situations may assist students in better preparing for work (Wendlandt and Rochlen, 2008). The RFT provides both an active learning environment where issues of transition, organizational culture, and professional ethics are discussed and significant fieldwork experience within the SLC.

Linking the Capstone Course, RFT, and Field Placement

The primary linkage between the capstone course, the RFT, and field place-ment is the research paper, described as a "senior thesis" in the Wagner Plan (Guarasci, 2006). In the senior psychology LC, the senior thesis is actually divided into two separate papers: one associated with their cap-stone course and the other with their RFT course. Students are challenged to connect historical concepts of a topic related to their field placement (in the capstone paper) with current research and reflection related to this same topic (in the RFT paper). In the capstone course, students are asked to write a review paper that serves as an opportunity to take a contempo-rary issue of controversy in psychology (preferably related to the RFT placement) and explore its historical roots. Students are encouraged to develop a thesis that is inspired or informed by their field placement expe-rience. At the time they submit a research proposal for evaluation, they have solidly been in their placement for several weeks. In a typical paper, the student will examine the development of theories and practice related to their field placement.

For example, a student who is placed in a clinical setting where a par-ticular form of psychotherapy is commonly employed may write a capstone paper on the origins of that particular approach, and questions about the efficacy of psychotherapy in general (and that method in particular). A student who interns in an advertisement agency may write a paper on the development of application of psychological research in advertisement and marketing. A student in biopsychology may write on the development of techniques used to measure whole brain activity in relation to psy-chological phenomena while placed at a local state neuroscience laboratory. Education students are encouraged to use their classroom teaching experi-ence as a point of departure. A typical education student may have a topic such as the origins of behavioral techniques used in classroom management or the development of theories regarding student learning styles.

In our most recent attempts to strengthen the connections between the capstone course, RFT, and field experience in the LC, modifications have been made to both the RFT and capstone papers. We now ask students to write a brief reflective "epilogue" to their capstone research paper to dis-cuss explicitly what they saw as connections (or not) between the RFT placement and the paper topic. This reflection also gives students an oppor-tunity to describe their field placement activities more fully to their cap-stone professor. In the RFT, students were originally required to complete an extensive review of recent (within the last decade) literature on their topic. However, John Dewey reminds us that one of the most important aspects of learning by doing is careful reflection (Stuckart and Glanz, 2010). Hence, the RFT paper was changed to a hybrid of scientific litera-ture review and critical reflection. Students are now required to write an extensive reflective paper relating to the field placement that integrates research throughout the paper.

Assessment of SLC

The Senior Program is overseen by the faculty who teach in the program, who meet periodically each year with the dean of integrated learning in the Senior Learning Community Council. Together they engage in extensive discussion regarding the Senior Program mission, best practices in SLC, standards, and assessment, among other topics. Together, this body developed a set of minimal requirements to which all departments are asked to adhere. However, unlike the first year and intermediate LCs, which are assessed using campuswide criteria, due to the variety in, and the discipline-specific nature of SLCs, the body decided to leave SLC assessment to departments (which all engage in periodic assessments of all academic programs they support). Thus, the only campuswide assessment of SLCs is included in the periodic assessment of the entire Wagner Plan, which is overseen by the Committee for Learning Assessment.

Since inception of the plan in 1998, various tools have been used to measure the LCs. Unfortunately, no pre–Wagner Plan assessment data are available to allow comparisons between the curriculum models. Tools employed by Wagner in the past included participation in the Collegiate Learning Assessment (CLA). Dissatisfaction with that measure (because of questions regarding its "fit" to Wagner) led to the creation of an in-house assessment tool based on Critical Thinking for Civic Thinking (CT^2; http://www4.ncsu.edu/~damcconn/ct2intro.html), which assesses writing, civic thinking, critical thinking, and experiential learning. The new tool, administered to students in the first year and senior year, will allow us to evaluate how students develop over their tenure at Wagner. No data are yet available from this new measure. Wagner has also participated in the National Survey of Student Engagement (NSSE) since 2001. There has been steady improvement in Wagner's standing on the NSSE; in the recently released 2010–11 academic year results, Wagner College first- and fourth-year students scored significantly higher in active and collaborative learning, student–faculty interaction, and enriching educational experiences when compared to comparable institutions (http://www.usatoday.com/news /education/nsse.htm). Information from these assessment tools is disseminated to faculty teaching SLCs through the Senior Learning Community Council and department chairs.

Each department uses its own method to assess the SLC. In the psychology department, we have developed a rubric that assesses how well the courses are meeting the standards set forth in the department's mission statement. In the SLC, a structured verbal assessment is used to gather feedback from students about their experiences, and it is this assessment process that has resulted in the modifications to the SLC courses described in previous sections of this chapter. Since its development ten years ago, the SLC has undergone several modifications in response to student and faculty feedback. In response to faculty and student concerns, the option to do independent laboratory-based research in place of a field placement was discontinued. The major concern was that these few students were not well integrated into the RFT discussions, which very frequently concerned issues associated with the field experience. Students can still engage in independent research outside the SLC through an independent study course that is supervised by a department professor. In addition, student feedback regarding time available for field placements has led to improved coordinated offerings of the RFT and capstone course (both courses are now taught on the same days of the week). Their suggestions have also led to improved consistency between thesis paper requirements and student assessment across different sections of the SLC and have led to the inclusion of a reflective writing piece where the student describes how their fieldwork is related (or not) to the research conducted in history of psychology. Finally, for the past five years, RFT students have been asked to provide a written assessment of the organizations in which they have their field experience. This process has allowed us to determine which organizations best meet our department's needs and improve the matching of subsequent students to field placements.

Unlike the entry-level C-BLCs described in Chapter Two, the SLC, due to its nature as a fourth-year program, has not been assessed for the level of social engagement fostered, or for its effect on retention. At the SLC level, many students know each other by virtue of having enrolled in several classes together previously and, very frequently, the faculty teaching in the SLC also know all of the students enrolled in the LC. The SLC should probably be assessed as a student retention factor; it is likely that a strong senior-year experience that is well advertised and attractive to students could act to keep students on track early in their academic career and may be as important to retention as first-year programs (Gardner and Van der Veer, 1998).

Lessons Learned

Our LC model enrolls students who are in their final year of college and are on the brink of entering their professional lives. Instead of transitioning students into college, we are transitioning them out of college. In our LC, students enroll in a cumulative capstone disciplinary course, as well as a reflective tutorial, and engage in a community-based field experience. This model (often modified in other departments to best meet the needs of students in a particular discipline as described earlier) is used in all academic departments at Wagner College, which illustrates its viability in all disciplines (for a description of all senior LCs, see http://www.wagner.edu/media/node/39). We can also envision its application to other courses that include experiential learning requirements (field experience, service learning, laboratory sections, and so on). Our classes are relatively small, but our model could work well for institutions with large capstone sections; each course could be linked to several smaller RFT sections, for example.

In our experience, it can be a challenge to connect the capstone course to the RFT and field placement. In addition to the assessment described previously, experience in linking course content to experiential learning gained from teaching first-year LCs was instrumental in the creation of the SLC. We have strengthened the connections by (1) including discussion of readings in the RFT that refer to the content of the capstone (in our case, contemporary writings on the impact of historical trends), (2) including discussion of readings in the capstone that refer to contemporary debates in the discipline, (3) having students more explicitly connect their disciplinary capstone research project to their field placement, and (4) having students explicitly connect their professional goals with their field placement and LC research work. We believe that it is critical for the professors teaching the components of the LC to share ideas regularly even when the course is not being taught. Many of the readings for the course developed not through formal planned meetings but organically through informal discussions. For example, we shared readings that we came across in our personal research or in a recent newspaper article and discussed how they could be beneficial for our students or could generate discussion of contemporary issues in psychology. The fact that we have taught the LC together annually for five years has enabled us to develop the course in a sustainable way, to make gradual modifications in response to each set of students, and to keep what works and eject what does not.

Teaching in the SLC is quite different from teaching in the first-year LC that has become popular on many campuses. Challenges of teaching in the first-year LC include disparities in student preparedness and motivation, explaining to students an unfamiliar curriculum and the values of experiential interdisciplinary learning, integrating students socially who are often living away from home for the first time, and assisting students to connect with the college. However, the LC provides opportunity for closer social and professional bonds, and the experience of watching high school students begin to turn into adult college students both intellectually and personally is high reward. In the SLC, the challenge is to take these (now more mature) college students and get them thinking more about life after college and how it is related to their chosen field of study. There remains an unevenness to their level of preparation and motivation for this next transition as well. Although many students are eager to move on, it is not uncommon for others to express to us that they are reluctant to leave school (indicative of the anxiety described by Wendlandt and Rochlen, 2008). The diversity of placements in which the students are engaged can make it difficult to find readings and foster discussion with wide application. The reward is in seeing them connecting the knowledge they have accumulated from their coursework in the major and from the general education curriculum with the fieldwork experience and discussions of the profession. Finally, it is always a pleasure to see the bonds that have developed among the senior students, some of which were formed in first-year LCs.

This LC, like all courses, is a work in progress. The diversity of student interests in, for example, careers and postbaccalaureate study, means that it is not possible to superimpose the previous year's template onto the next class. Furthermore, because we are attempting to transition students out of their undergraduate experience, faculty must (in conjunction with college career development offices) keep an eye on changing interests and needs of community organizations, professional schools, and even economic opportunities. According to Hensheid (2008), senior programs that link the undergraduate curriculum to life after graduation can help students find jobs, make connections, strengthen links between different learning outcomes from first year to last, and create a sense of community among seniors. LCs can be used to provide effective support for the transition from college to career, as they have for students moving from high school to college.

References

Bay, J. "Preparing Undergraduates for Careers: An Argument for the Internship Practicum." *College English*, 2006, *69*(2), 134–141.

Chickering, A. W., and Schlossberg, N. K. "Moving on: Seniors as People in Transition." In J. N. Gardner and G. Van der Veer (eds), *The Senior Year Experience: Facilitating Integration, Reflection, Closure, and Transition*. San Francisco: Jossey-Bass, 1998.

Gardner, J. N., and Van der Veer, G. "A Summary Agenda for Enriching the Senior Year." In J. N. Gardner and G. Van der Veer (eds), *The Senior Year Experience: Facilitating Integration, Reflection, Closure, and Transition*. San Francisco: Jossey-Bass, 1998.

Guarasci, R. "On the Challenge of Becoming the Good College." *Liberal Education*, 2006, *92*(1), 14–21.

Hensheid, J. M. "Preparing Seniors for Life after College." *Open Campus*, 2008 (Nov.–Dec.), 21–25.

Lenning, O. T., and Ebbers, L. H. *The Powerful Potential of Learning Communities: Improving Education for the Future*. ASHE-ERIC Higher Education Report, Vol. 26, No. 6. Washington, D.C.: George Washington University, 1999.

Light, A. "Job Mobility and Wage Growth: Evidence from the NLSY79." *Monthly Labor Review*, 2005, *128*(2), 33–39.

Stuckart, D. W., and Glanz, J. *Revisiting Dewey: Best Practices for Educating the Whole Child Today*. Lanham, Md.: Rowman and Littlefield Education, 2010.

Wagner College, 2011a. "What Is the Senior Learning Community?" Retrieved June 2, 2011, from http://www.wagner.edu/media/node/38.

Wagner College, 2011b. "Psychology Senior Program." Retrieved June 2, 2011, from http://www.wagner.edu/media/node/58.

Wendlandt, N. M., and Rochlen, A. B. "Addressing the College-to-Work Transition." *Journal of College Development*, 2008, *35*(2), 151–165.

Zimbardo, P. G. "Does Psychology Make a Significant Difference in Our Lives?" *American Psychologist*, 2004, *59*(5), 339–351.

LAURENCE J. NOLAN and STEVE M. JENKINS are professor and associate professor of psychology, respectively, at Wagner College and have taught the senior learning community together for five years. Both have taught first-year and senior learning communities, and Nolan has also taught in the intermediate LC. For three years Jenkins was chair of the senior LC council, which is a body composed of faculty from all disciplines at Wagner College that meets regularly to discuss standards and best practices of the senior LC.

NEW DIRECTIONS FOR TEACHING AND LEARNING • DOI: 10.1002/tl

4

This chapter describes the Psychology Early Awareness Program (PEAP) at Loyola Marymount University, a residential learning community centered within a discipline. We discuss the theory that supports the value of living-learning communities, describe how this guided the development of PEAP, and summarize the benefits of this approach.

Residential Learning Communities Centered Within a Discipline: The Psychology Early Awareness Program

Cheryl N. Grills, Adam W. Fingerhut, Vandana Thadani, Ricardo Arturo Machón

Learning communities have increasingly become a mechanism for education reform in elementary, secondary, and postsecondary education. Recognizing that learning occurs both inside and outside the classroom, their emergence is partly a response to the critique that undergraduate education at American research universities lacks integrated and focused student learning (Boyer Commission on Educating Undergraduates in the Research University, 1998; Pike, 1999). In other words, the typical college experience for many students is a solitary one, with each student selecting and taking separate, often disconnected courses; living in dormitories with peers who may or may not share career or intellectual interests; and engaging in extracurricular activities that are likewise disconnected from what is occurring in the classroom and in the dorm. Within higher education, learning communities allow for integration of students' academic (or intellectual) and social experiences—with the idea that ultimately such an integration enhances academic performance, engagement, and retention (Li, McCoy, Shelley, and Whalen, 2005).

Since their emergence in educational settings, learning communities as a means of integrating students' academic and social experiences have taken a number of forms: as structures *inside* classrooms that facilitate student learning of particular skills or content areas through collaborations

NEW DIRECTIONS FOR TEACHING AND LEARNING, no. 132, Winter 2012 © Wiley Periodicals, Inc.
Published online in Wiley Online Library (wileyonlinelibrary.com) • DOI: 10.1002/tl.20035

with their peers (Brown, 1997; see also Chapter Five in this volume), as on-line collaborations that engage students in academic projects by connecting youth across the world (for example, see iEARN at www.iearn.org; see also Chapter Seven in this volume), and as vehicles for connecting students and faculty with similar interests (see Chapter Six). Many learning communities attempt to create connections between students and faculty and the curriculum (Smith, MacGregor, Mathews, and Gabelnick, 2004; see also Chapters Two and Three). When these efforts attempt to extend these connections beyond the classroom and into the residence halls, they are referred to as living-learning communities or as residential learning communities, which are the focus of this chapter.

Definition and Theoretical Foundations of Residential Learning Communities

According to Brower and Inkelas (2010), residential learning communities are "housing programs that incorporate academically based themes and build community through common learning" (p. 36). Such communities began as early as the 1920s (Rocheleau, Smith, Bergman, and Zrull, 2011) and were born out of the assumption that education works best when curricular and cocurricular activities are linked, when students' social experiences are integrated into the larger academic and intellectual context. Such an assumption fits nicely with a relational model of human development (Covington and Surrey, 1997; Gilligan, 1982; Jordan and others, 1991). In this context human development is viewed as growth and connections with and toward others. Healthy connection with others (rather than autonomous disconnection) is the means toward and the goal of psychological development. It is also the foundation for growth, intellectual development, and achievement in life.

From this perspective, academic success is connected to relational developmental processes. As students are able to nurture student–student relationships and connections to a disciplinary interest and faculty associated with that discipline, they grow socially and intellectually. Subsequently, students' commitments to their undergraduate institution, their chosen major, and career trajectory are strengthened. Furthermore, the model speaks to the importance of students' roles in the learning community context: students in these communities must not only take on responsibility for their own learning but for others in the community as well; they must develop greater interdependence with, understanding of, and empathy for their peers (Brown, 1997; Riel and Fulton, 2001). The resulting healthy connections with others are "mutual, creative, energy-releasing, and empowering for all participants, and are fundamental to ... psychological well-being" (Covington and Surrey, 1997, p. 337).

Empirical evidence suggests both intellectual and social benefits of residential learning communities. Participation in residential learning communities has been associated with positive student outcomes, including better critical-thinking skills, higher rates of civic engagement, and easier transition to college (Brower and Inkelas, 2010). In addition, most studies of residential learning communities show that, in comparison to students in traditional residence halls, those in learning communities report higher grades (Barron, Buch, Andre, and Spaulding, 2010; Pascarella, Terenzini, and Blimling, 1994). In a study by Brower (2008), students who participated in a residential learning community consumed less alcohol and experienced fewer negative outcomes associated with drinking than those in more traditional dorm settings.

It is important to note that residential learning communities are not monolithic. For example, though some residence-based programs are managed by administrators in student affairs or housing, others are managed by academic affairs or faculty from a particular department. In addition, whereas some programs require that students enroll in shared classes, others do not. In an analysis of over 600 different residential learning communities, Brower and Inkelas (2010) identified more than a dozen categories of such communities. Examples include residence-based programs focused on a shared political interest; programs aimed at female students, first-year students, or second-year students; and programs targeting social, cultural, or civic interests.

In undergraduate education, the most recent advancements have taken the form of residential learning communities that operate within the context of specific academic disciplines. Typically, these incorporate activities that foster engaged, collaborative learning and participation through educational and social activities that extend beyond the classroom and that allow students to draw upon a variety of sources to engage in a focused study of a discipline. Next, we share a brief sampling of residential learning communities centered on psychology from around the country. Then we provide an in-depth example of the residential learning community that we developed at Loyola Marymount University (LMU).

Starting in the fall of 2002, James Madison University (JMU) created a residential learning community targeting approximately twenty first-year students interested in psychology. In addition to a residential component in which all student participants live in the same dorm, students are also required to take several linked courses together. Specifically, students enroll in special sections of two research methods courses (one in the fall and one in the spring) and in a course designed to teach students about the discipline of psychology and the different opportunities within the discipline. The program goals were inspired by the American Psychological Association's 10 learning goals for undergraduate majors and by Astin's (1993) suggestion that student–student interactions, student–faculty interactions, and time spent on task are the best predictors of college success. To date the program is having great success: students in the program report higher grade point average (GPA), both in the major and overall, than other psychology students (Barron, Buch, Andre, and Spaulding, 2010).

Another example of a residential learning community, once again linked to psychology, comes from Appalachian State University (ASU; the curricular component of this LC has already been described in Chapter Two.) One of the unique pieces about ASU's program, Brain Matters, is that it is not exclusively for students who want to major in psychology. Instead, it is for students interested in the field regardless of whether it is their primary intellectual or academic interest or not. Similar to JMU's program, ASU requires students to live together and take classes together and co-curricular programming is intimately tied to course content and to the residential component. For example, faculty involved in Brain Matters host office hours in the dorm. Though data have yet to be reported on this particular community, data from other residential learning communities on the same campus demonstrate great benefits to the students and to the university including significantly higher retention rates.

The Context and Origins of LMU's Residential Learning Community

Loyola Marymount University began implementing themed living–learning communities in deliberate efforts to maximize academic engagement and promote sustained student retention and academic success. LMU is a student-centered, Jesuit–Marymount university located in Los Angeles whose mission is the encouragement of learning, the education of the whole person, the service of faith, and the promotion of justice. Within this broader university mission, the Department of Psychology aims to develop ethical leaders for a culturally diverse world and to contribute to the liberal education of its majors. Through a comprehensive education in the science of psychology, the department's curriculum is committed to educating the whole person, the pursuit of academic excellence, advancing scholarship, promoting service and justice, and encouraging lifelong learning.

In 2008, the Psychology Department established a residential learning community for entering first-year psychology majors called the Psychology Early Awareness Program (PEAP). Following Life Sciences, PEAP was the second academically driven residential learning community at LMU. PEAP most closely approximates Lenning and Ebbers's (1999) residential learning community, yet it contains features of their curriculum-based learning community with linked courses and embedded cohort models (see Chapters Two and Three). We were inspired to create the program based on our belief that learning does not and should not end when class is over. As Davis and Murrell (1993) have suggested, "for growth to occur, the work that is done in the classroom must find expression in other aspects of a student's life" (p. 286).

PEAP was conceived as a residential learning community in particular because we strongly believed that this structure could optimize students' ability to navigate the transition to college. Entering college is similar to a rite of passage (Van Gennep, 1960). Students go through a process of separation, transition, and incorporation. Although rites of passage may occur many times during a student's career, the first year is particularly important (Pike and others, 1997). Given this, PEAP is designed so that first-year psychology majors live together in a designated residence hall, participate in coordinated curricular activities, and have access to other academic programs and services. In-class and out-of-class experiences are linked, creating a seamless, integrated educational environment focused on learning, academic success, and personal development.

PEAP was designed to promote the university and department's mission and vision through a student-centered immersion process. To do this we used the best of what is known about residential learning communities. Brower and Inkelas (2010) identified three characteristics that are associated with the most successful residential learning communities. To begin, successful programs detail clear learning objectives with a strong academic focus. Central to this is the inclusion of at least one course that students in the program are required to take together as well as academically based activities that occur alongside regular coursework. Second, successful programs take advantage of community settings to create learning opportunities. Third, successful programs require a strong, clear relationship between the leaders of the program, including both academic and student affairs. In addition to these qualities, PEAP was inspired by four characteristics that Jerome Bruner identified through his observations of one learning community (Brown, 1997). These include:

> agency: taking more control of your mental activity…; reflection: not simply "learning in the raw" but making what you learn make sense.…; collaboration: sharing the resources of the mix of human beings involved in teaching and learning…; [and] culture, the way of life and thought that we construct, negotiate, institutionalize, and finally…end up by calling reality… (Bruner, 1996, as cited in Brown, 1997, p. 399).

Reflecting these principles, our goals for the program are as follows. PEAP students should:

- Feel a sense of community, bonding, and engagement to peers, faculty, the broader educational community, and the field of psychology.
- Feel supported by peers, faculty, and the broader university community.
- Feel a sense of engagement in classes.
- Take responsibility for their own learning and that of their peers.
- Use collaboration and teaming strategies to enhance their educational potential.

NEW DIRECTIONS FOR TEACHING AND LEARNING • DOI: 10.1002/tl

- Value opportunities for exploration and value intellectual pursuits in higher education.
- Demonstrate greater awareness of available resources at the university and greater knowledge of how to access them.
- Demonstrate improved academic outcomes, as evidenced by GPA in both their major and LMU's core courses and through higher retention rates.

The Design and Implementation of PEAP

On average, the Department of Psychology receives approximately eighty entering first-year psychology majors who are invited during summer orientation to enroll in the PEAP learning community. The program allots only twenty-five slots, accommodating a little less than one-third of the fall first-year class. Although students self-select into PEAP, attention is given to achieving gender and ethnic diversity in the program admission process.

The Residential Component. As discussed previously, learning communities offer not only an opportunity for intellectual integration across courses but also for social integration. To maximize this potential, participants in PEAP live together on one floor of a highly sought-after freshmen dormitory with an assigned resident advisor who is also a psychology major. Participants begin the program the week prior to the start of fall classes to participate in three days of bonding, engaged learning, and local Los Angeles excursions. In addition to helping students connect with one another, this immersion component is designed to introduce participants to different experiences and opportunities available through LMU and the city of Los Angeles. PEAP students immerse themselves in diverse communities facing concrete challenges that heighten social awareness and inspire lifelong social action. During the year, monthly informal "fireside chats" with department faculty occur within the dorm setting. This provides PEAP students a chance to get to know and develop relationships with department faculty, upper-class students, and PEAP alumni. Within these chats, students learn about faculty research, careers in psychology, and getting into graduate school. In addition, and perhaps more importantly, these chats provide a space for students to discuss current hot topics in psychology. Students rarely have this type of access to faculty and professionals in the field at this stage of their college career.

Finally, in the Spring Semester, students engage in a Spring Event Weekend activity. These are specially designed, psychology-focused "alternative break" opportunities exclusively for PEAP participants. These activities promote service and cultural exchange on the local and national levels through hands-on, community-based learning during academic-year breaks. Through PEAP, our students engage with individuals outside the LMU community and integrate with the larger world in which they live. Spring Event activities have included service-learning activities at a

NEW DIRECTIONS FOR TEACHING AND LEARNING • DOI: 10.1002/tl

women's prison, engagement with youth community organizers in economically challenged inner-city neighborhoods, participation in community campaigns in the skid row community, and discussion and sharing with formerly incarcerated youth involved in juvenile justice campaigns. Most recently an activity included a visit to a Los Angeles school, serving large numbers of English-language-learners and low socio-economic-status children in an intervention effort involving literacy and reading motivation.

The Academic Component. All entering first-year psychology majors are required to take Introductory Psychology for majors. In addition, they are all required to enroll in "core" courses in philosophy, math, science, and English. With that in mind and with the intention of creating a truly integrated intellectual experience, the PEAP schedule is coordinated by the Dean's Office, Psychology Department, English Department, Math Department, Philosophy Department, and Life Sciences Department. Designated sections of required foundational courses expected of all first-semester psychology students are reserved for PEAP students only.

The first-semester English class is linked thematically and academically to the Introductory Psychology course, and Introductory Psychology is also linked to a one-unit liberal arts course focused on personal and academic development. The resulting fall semester PEAP schedule is preset, and all PEAP learning community students rotate together through classes that are open only to them. In addition, once the semester begins, resident advisors who work with the PEAP students coordinate group study sessions in the dorms so that students can collaborate with one another and to further create a total "learning community." Careful coordination and collaboration across divisions (Student Affairs and Academic Affairs), across departments (Psychology, English, Math, Philosophy, and Science), and with local community-based organizations is required to set up the coordinated curricula and cocurricular program. Resource sharing and participatory planning has been essential to establish the multifaceted nature of the program.

Examining the Effectiveness of PEAP

A necessary component of the program includes an examination of its potential effectiveness. Thus, we conducted a study that compared the academic performance of PEAP students with a comparison group of nonparticipants. We gathered data from two sources. First, we collaborated with Loyola Marymount University's institutional research department in order to compare classroom performance and retention rates for PEAP participants versus non-PEAP psychology students. Second, we surveyed PEAP participants in order to hear about their experience in their own words. The overall PEAP sample included forty-two students who participated in either the first or second year of the program, twenty-three from 2008–2009 and nineteen from 2009–2010. The comparison sample included 198

Table 4.1. Means and Standard Deviations for Self-Report Items

		M	SD
To what extent did your participation in PEAP help you DEVELOP A SENSE OF...	Connection with peers in the psychology major	4.59	.71
	Belonging with psychology faculty	4.19	1.00
	Support from peers	4.50	.72
	Connectedness with the field of psychology	4.28	.89
	Engagement in classes	4.03	1.00
	Responsibility for your own learning	3.88	.98
To what extent did your participation in PEAP help you DEVELOP AN ABILITY TO...	Synthesize and apply a variety of learning techniques	3.59	1.04
	Think critically about psychology	4.16	.88
	Think critically about scientific research	3.66	1.00
	Succeed academically (for example, in terms of GPA)	3.72	1.11
To what extent did your participation in PEAP help you...	Develop an awareness of the university's resources	4.03	.90
	Develop an intrinsic appreciation of learning	3.84	.99
	Value intellectual pursuits in higher education	4.16	.99
	Value participation in outside of class discussions	4.09	.93

students who completed the Psychology 101 course, an Introductory Psychology class for those who are declared psychology majors, from the fall of 2006 through the fall of 2009.

Our results suggest that PEAP is having a positive impact on student retention: 100 percent of PEAP participants returned for their second academic year, compared with 81 percent of comparison students. These differences persisted beyond the second year as well. For those who had Junior year data 91 percent of PEAP students were retained, whereas 68 percent in the comparison group were retained. In terms of grades and GPA, the data were less clear. PEAP students statistically outperformed comparison students on only one of five first-semester courses. Specifically, PEAP students scored significantly higher in their Philosophy course, a course that focuses on critical-thinking skills, but there were no differences in Introductory Psychology, First-Year English, Statistics, or Natural Science. However, the PEAP participants' overall GPA at the end of the first semester, at the end of the first year, and the end of the second year was slightly higher than that of the comparison group, though none of the relationships was statistically significant.

The self-report data allowed us to more fully examine the effectiveness of PEAP and our ability to accomplish our stated goals. In general, participants reported receiving great benefit from the program. For example, almost all participants (93.8 percent) reported that PEAP helped them "quite a lot" to "very much" in developing a sense of support from peers. In addition, in terms of collaboration and community, 87.5 percent of participants stated that PEAP helped them "quite a lot" to "very much" in developing a sense of connection with peers in the major, 78.9 percent in sense of belonging with psychology faculty, and 84.4 percent in developing connection with the field of psychology. Comments made in response to the open-ended prompts corroborate these data. One student, for example, wrote the following:

> I was very grateful for the sense of community that was created. I really got to know and love all of my peers quickly. Even now I have a strong bond with my PEAPs. Also, I became close with a lot of the faculty. This made asking questions and getting help so much less scary.

Another student wrote, "I enjoyed having classes the first semester with my friends and the people I lived with. Being in PEAP enabled me to develop friendships quickly."

In terms of agency, 81.3 percent reported that PEAP helped them "quite a lot" to "very much" in taking responsibility for their learning, 71.9 percent in developing an intrinsic appreciation for learning, 81.3 percent in valuing intellectual pursuits, and 78.1 percent in valuing out-of-class discussions. In terms of reflection, 84.4 percent used the top two answer choices to indicate that PEAP helped them think critically about psychology; a smaller number (62.6 percent) indicated that PEAP helped them think critically about scientific research. Once again, statements from the PEAP students help to flesh out these numbers. One student wrote, "I am unafraid to take on difficult academic aspirations because I know I have my PEAP community and faculty to fall back on should I need to," whereas other students wrote that participation in PEAP helped "strengthen my passion for psychology" and "connecting real world experiences with my current educational pursuits." Interestingly, and in line with the institutional data, only 59.4 percent stated that PEAP had helped them "quite a lot" to "very much" in succeeding academically in terms of grades.

Lessons Learned and Recommendations

PEAP was created at LMU as way to provide a subset of first-year psychology majors with a comprehensive educational experience that would allow them to develop intellectually and personally. Data collected from the first two years of the program suggest that we have been successful on several fronts. Most clearly, PEAP helped students connect to the university, the major, and to their peers. The data on the academic component of the program were less clear. Though students in PEAP outperformed comparison students on some dimensions, the effects were not so consistent or so robust as we would expect. In addition, students reported mixed feelings about the comprehensive nature of the intellectual experience we have created and implemented. On one hand, many students reported benefitting from taking classes together in their first semester and being able to rely on each other in their hallway for help with studying; simultaneously, they reported feeling relatively isolated from other first-year students given that all their courses are linked at the start of the school year.

Now that two years of the program have been completed and the data have been analyzed, we are able to reflect on the lessons learned and the limitations of the project. To begin, how did the program stack up to its theoretical underpinnings? First, we saw evidence of a community that incorporated the four elements identified by Bruner—collaboration, through formal (that is, program-delivered) and informal (for example, student study groups) structures (Brown, 1997). Students evidenced agency over not only their own but their peers' learning as well. Several of the events (for example, fireside chats) incorporated "physical spaces" for reflection and sharing. And ultimately, these resulted in a culture of learning, support, and integration of students' academic–intellectual and social worlds that were different from what we have observed among our non-PEAP majors. Furthermore, consistent with the relational model of development, students' self reports suggested the development of relationships with peers and faculty was the glue underlying many of the program's successes (Covington and Surrey, 1997; Gilligan, 1982; Jordan and others, 1991). Finally, the higher retention rates that we observed suggest that our decision to target first-year students, who face potentially challenging transitions on entering college, was a sound one.

From a pragmatic perspective, the past two years have revealed ways in which PEAP can be further strengthened to more deliberately achieve our goals. First, we recognize that we need to clarify what components are central to a living–learning community. Though we were clear on the importance of academic and social integration, we may have, ironically, failed to meaningfully integrate these two pieces as successfully as we could have. For example, it appears that little intellectual programming occurred in the dorm and that the blending of living and learning may not have been achieved. In the current iteration of the program, the psychology faculty who serve as codirectors for PEAP are deliberately coordinating with student housing staff and resident advisors to ensure that students are truly engaging in dialogue about their learning within their home environment. Furthermore, the programming in the dorm will move beyond study sessions, to drive students to take ownership over their own intellectual development. In addition, using surveys of prior PEAP students, we have determined that fewer linked courses will likely be more effective than our earlier fully linked-schedule model. Thus the most recent cohort of PEAP students is slated, in the fall semester, to take their Introductory

Psychology, English, and 1-unit liberal arts courses together, and in the Spring semester to take their Brain and Behavior course together.

Another issue that has arisen since the initiation of PEAP concerns equity issues among our students. A residential learning community necessarily requires dedicating valuable and limited resources to a small group of individuals. Some have questioned whether this is fair and whether it puts our other students at a disadvantage. Recognizing that this is a real issue, we are intentionally finding ways to have PEAP students give back to the "life" of the department as a way to maximize our "investment" (both financially and in terms of human resources). To date, this has happened organically as many former PEAP students have chosen to involve themselves in the department as a way to give to other students. For example, the current president of Psi Chi (our honors society) and the Villagers (our student-run organization) are PEAP alums. In addition, many of the research assistants in the department were involved in the program. As the program continues, we will remain cognizant of balancing the rewards given to the PEAP participants in contrast to our other majors.

As a final lesson learned, it is clear that buy-in is needed from many constituencies and that, for the program to succeed, ongoing collaboration and relationship building with these constituencies must occur. Though the program has an academic focus and is housed in the Psychology Department, it cannot function effectively without close working relationships with Student Affairs and with buy-in from a cross section of units in the university. The program works best when there is a team of committed people across divisions and departments with a vested interest in its success. In addition, the program works best when everyone in the department is involved. Because the particular type of residential learning community that we created is centered in an academic department, all the faculty in that department must be on board and willing to be involved. In our own experience, such involvement took the form of participating in fireside chats in the dorm and in attending events off campus with students during the opening weekend of the school year and the Alternative Weekend. More can be done, however. For example, ongoing communication with the faculty needs to occur so that they are abreast of the workings of the program and of the students enrolled, and so they can have a voice in making the program more effective.

In addition to considering the lessons learned, we are also clear that more research needs to be done to better understand the residential learning community experience. For example, though we are aware that these processes work and are effective in helping students academically and personally, data are needed to examine the mechanisms by which specific practices achieve their effects on student outcomes including their academic success and their sense of community and social integration. In addition, more needs to be known about how the institutional context in which residential learning communities occur moderates the effectiveness of the

NEW DIRECTIONS FOR TEACHING AND LEARNING • DOI: 10.1002/tl

programs. In our own case, for example, it is likely that some of the specific pieces of PEAP worked, in part, because they were aligned with the university's mission. Specifically, students responded quite well to events where they interacted with community members and with people on the margins of society; this is perfectly in line with the university's mission to educate individuals in the promotion of social justice. Future research should examine facets of the specific institutional context that can serve as barriers or supports in achieving the goals of the living–learning community.

References

Astin, A. W. *What Matters in College? Four Critical Years Revisited.* San Francisco: Jossey-Bass, 1993.

Barron, K. E., Buch, K. K., Andre, J. T., and Spaulding, S. *Best Practices for Teaching Beginnings and Endings in the Psychology Major.* New York: Oxford University Press, 2010.

Boyer Commission on Educating Undergraduates in the Research University. *Reinventing Undergraduate Education: A Blueprint for America's Research Universities.* Stony Brook: State University of New York, 1998.

Brower, A. M. "More Like a Home than a Hotel: The Impact of Living-Learning Programs on College High-Risk Drinking." *Journal of College and University Student Housing,* 2008, *35*(1), 32–49.

Brower, A. M., and Inkelas, K. K. "Living-Learning Programs: One High-Impact Educational Practice We Now Know a Lot About." *Liberal Education,* 2010, *96*(2), 36–43.

Brown, A. L. "Transforming Schools into Communities of Thinking and Learning About Serious Matters." *American Psychologist,* 1997, *52*, 399–413.

Covington, S. S., and Surrey, J. L. "The Relational Model of Women's Psychological Development: Implications for Substance Abuse." In S. Wilsnack and R. Wilsnack (eds.), *Gender and Alcohol: Individual and Social Perspectives.* New Brunswick, N.J.: Rutgers Center of Alcohol Studies, 1997.

Davis, T. M., & Murrell, P. H. "A Structural Model of Perceived Academic, Personal, and Vocational Gains Related to College Student Responsibility." *Research in Higher Education,* 1993, *34*, 267–290.

Gilligan, C. *In a Different Voice: Psychological Theory and Women's Development.* Cambridge, Mass.: Harvard University Press, 1982.

Jordan, J. V., and others. *Women's Growth in Connection: Writings from the Stone Center.* New York: Guilford Press, 1991.

Lenning, O. T., and Ebbers, L. H. *The Powerful Potential of Learning Communities: Improving Education for the Future.* ASHE-ERIC Higher Education Report, Vol. 26, No. 6. Washington, D.C.: Graduate School of Education and Human Development, George Washington University, 1999.

Li, Y., McCoy, E., Shelley, M. C., and Whalen, D. F. "Student Satisfaction with Special Program (Fresh Start) Residence Halls." *Journal of College Student Development,* 2005, *46*(2), 176–192.

Pascarella, E. T., Terenzini, P. T., and Blimling, G. S. "The Impact of Residential Life on Students." In C. C. Schroeder and P. Mable (eds.), *Realizing the Educational Potential of Residence Halls* (pp. 22–52). San Francisco: Jossey-Bass, 1994.

Pike, G. R. "The Effects of Residential Learning Communities and Traditional Residential Living Arrangements on Educational Gains During the First Year of College." *Journal of College Student Development,* 1999, *40*(3), 269–282.

Pike, G. R., Schroeder, C. C., and Berry, T. R. "Enhancing the Educational Impact of Residence Halls: The Relationship Between Residential Learning Communities and First-Year Experiences and Persistence." *Journal of College Student Development*, 1997, *38*(6), 609–620.

Riel, M., and Fulton, K. "The Role of Technology in Supporting Learning Communities." *Phi Delta Kappan*, 2001, *82*, 518–523.

Rocheleau, C. A., Smith, M. C., Bergman, S., and Zrull, M. C. "Residential Learning Communities in Psychology: How to Get Started." In R. L. Miller, and others (eds.), *Promoting Student Engagement. Vol. 1: Programs, Techniques and Opportunities.* Washington, D.C.: Society for Teaching Psychology, 2011. Retrieved May 31, 2011, from http://teachpsych.org/resources/e-books/pse2011/vol1/.

Smith, B. L., MacGregor, J., Mathews, R. S., and Gabelnick, F. *Learning Communities: Reforming Undergraduate Education.* San Francisco: Jossey-Bass, 2004.

Van Gennep, A. *The Rites of Passage* (M. Vizedon and G. Caffee, Trans.). Chicago: The University of Chicago Press, 1960.

CHERYL N. GRILLS *is a professor in the Department of Psychology and associate dean in the College of Liberal Arts at Loyola Marymount University.*

ADAM W. FINGERHUT *is an assistant professor in the Department of Psychology at Loyola Marymount University.*

VANDANA THADANI *is an associate professor in the Department of Psychology and faculty associate at the Center for Teaching Excellence at Loyola Marymount University.*

RICARDO ARTURO MACHÓN *is a professor in the Department of Psychology at Loyola Marymount University.*

NEW DIRECTIONS FOR TEACHING AND LEARNING • DOI: 10.1002/tl

5

This chapter describes three approaches to creating classroom-based learning communities: interteaching; team-based learning; and cooperative learning in large, lecture-based courses.

Creating Learning Communities in the Classroom

Bryan K. Saville, Natalie Kerr Lawrence, Krisztina V. Jakobsen

Presumably as long as institutions of higher learning have been in existence, educators have attempted to identify ways that students could have more successful educational experiences. Starting in the late 1960s, however, the practice of identifying the factors that best predicted academic success in college became more systematic (Astin, 1973; Chickering, 1969; see also Kuh, 2001). Since that time, one factor that has been shown consistently to predict success in college is student engagement, which Astin (1984/1999) defined as "the amount of physical and psychological energy that the student devotes to the academic experience" (p. 518). In short, students who are more engaged in college, both in and out of the classroom, typically have more successful academic experiences than those who are less engaged (Astin, 1993; Pascarella and Terenzini, 1991).

Astin (1993) also identified three specific types of student engagement that best predict academic success: time on task, student–student interactions, and student–faculty interactions. Thus, students who spend more time interacting (both in and out of the classroom) with their course material, other students, and their instructors tend to perform better in their classes and have more positive academic experiences than students who spend less time doing these activities.

In addition to conducting research aimed at better understanding the relation between student engagement and academic success, educators have spent considerable time constructing pedagogical practices based on the theory that increasing student engagement produces positive outcomes

NEW DIRECTIONS FOR TEACHING AND LEARNING, no. 132, Winter 2012 © Wiley Periodicals, Inc.
Published online in Wiley Online Library (wileyonlinelibrary.com) • DOI: 10.1002/tl.20036

(Astin, 1993). One such practice that has received considerable attention in recent years is constructing learning communities (for example, Gamson, 2000; Lenning and Ebbers, 1999; Shapiro and Levine, 1999; Zhao and Kuh, 2004). Although Lenning and Ebbers (1999) identified several types of learning communities, each with its own subtypes (as covered in other chapters in this volume), here we are concerned with what they referred to as classroom-based learning communities.

There are two subtypes of classroom-based learning communities: total-classroom learning communities and within-classroom learning communities. Both of these subtypes have at their core cooperative learning and "a culture ... in which everyone is involved in a collective effort of understanding" (Bielaczyc and Collins, 1999, p. 271). Thus, most college classes, with their emphasis on lecture-based instructional methods and independent (that is, noncooperative) learning, do not meet the criteria for either type of classroom-based learning community even if students engage in a bit of "group work" from time to time (Lenning and Ebbers, 1999).

A good example of a total-classroom learning community would be an elementary-school classroom, in which the teacher and students work together, continuously and cooperatively, to maximize student learning (Lenning and Ebbers, 1999). Another example might be a small, graduate-level seminar in which the students and teacher work together in a collective fashion to enhance learning. Either way, total-classroom learning communities involve the entire class, students and teacher, working together as a "community" to improve learning.

In contrast, within-classroom learning communities entail smaller groups of students from a single class working together to improve each other's learning. Typically, group membership in within-classroom learning communities stays constant during a course. A nice example of a teaching method that creates within-classroom learning communities is problem-based learning (PBL), in which smaller groups of students work together to solve ill-defined problems that may have several different solutions (for example, Connor-Greene, 2005; Duch, Groh, and Allen, 2001).

Ultimately, there are many ways to construct classroom-based learning communities (see Lenning and Ebbers, 1999, for examples). Nevertheless, the emphasis is always on cooperative learning. In this chapter, we focus on three teaching methods—interteaching, team-based learning, and cooperative learning in large, lecture-based courses—that we have used successfully to create classroom-based learning communities in our psychology classes at James Madison University. As we discuss shortly, interteaching creates a total-classroom learning community. Team-based learning, in contrast, creates within-classroom communities but also provides the opportunity to create a total-classroom community. Finally, cooperative learning in lecture-based courses creates within-classroom learning communities. Although each of these methods is unique on the surface and in

NEW DIRECTIONS FOR TEACHING AND LEARNING • DOI: 10.1002/tl

terms of its philosophical underpinnings, each capitalizes on the benefits of cooperative learning and provides a way for instructors to create learning communities in their classrooms.

Interteaching

Interteaching is a multicomponent teaching method that has its philosophical roots in B. F. Skinner's operant psychology, or as it is often called these days, behavior analysis (Boyce and Hineline, 2002). A typical interteaching session works as follows (for more information, see Boyce and Hineline, 2002; Saville, Lambert, and Robertson, 2011). First, the instructor constructs a preparation (prep) guide, the purpose of which is to guide students through a reading assignment. The prep guides usually consist of anywhere from five to fifteen items, each of which may contain one or more related questions about a particular concept, and cover five to twenty pages of material, depending on difficulty of the material, how often the class meets, the goals of the instructor, and so on. The instructor distributes each prep guide several days in advance (often via a course website), and students complete it outside of class. Then during a typical class, students form pairs and spend approximately two-thirds of the class period discussing their answers to the prep-guide items and helping one another learn the material. Because the composition of the pairs changes frequently (see Boyce and Hineline, 2002), students typically work with many students during the semester. For this reason, interteaching may be considered an example of a total-classroom learning community. During the pair discussions, the instructor moves around the classroom, interacting with students, answering questions, and guiding their conversations. Once students have finished their discussions, they complete a record sheet on which they list, among other things, how well their discussion went, which items were difficult to understand, and any items they would like the instructor to review. Using this information, the instructor then prepares a brief lecture that targets the prep-guide items that most students had trouble understanding. The lecture begins the next period and precedes the next pair discussion.

In short, interteaching creates a unique total-classroom learning community, where two-thirds of a class is focused on cooperative learning and one-third is spent on focused lecturing by the instructor. Moreover, interteaching is practical for many types of classes. One of us has used interteaching in a wide variety of psychology courses, including Introductory Psychology, Research Methods, Psychology of Learning, History of Psychology, and several graduate-level psychology courses. Class size in these courses has ranged from as few as ten students to as many as eighty students. Interteaching has also been incorporated into computer science courses (Emurian and Zheng, 2010), sociology courses (Tsui, 2010), religion courses (Zeller, 2010), nutrition science courses (Goto and Schneider,

2010), and special education courses (Cannella-Malone, Axe, and Parker, 2009).

Research. Since Boyce and Hineline's (2002) introduction of interteaching, researchers have begun to examine its impact on student learning (for a review, see Saville and others, 2011). In the first analysis of interteaching, Saville, Zinn, and Elliott (2005) conducted a lab-based study in which they randomly assigned college students to one of three teaching conditions—interteaching, lecture, or reading—and exposed them to material from a short journal article. Saville and others then invited these students (along with students in a control condition who did not attend the first teaching session) back to the lab a week later to take a multiple-choice quiz over the material. Students in the interteaching condition scored significantly higher on the quiz than students in the other three conditions. Saville and others (2006) then compared interteaching to lecture in actual graduate (Study 1) and undergraduate (Study 2) courses. In both studies, students earned higher exam scores following interteaching sessions. Students also reported that they preferred interteaching to lecture.

Researchers have also examined how interteaching affects students' critical-thinking skills. Saville and others (2008) alternated between interteaching and lecture several times during a semester and found that students were more likely to report engaging in critical-thinking behaviors under the interteaching condition. In another study, Scoboria and Pascual-Leone (2009) exposed students to an "interteaching-like" method or lecture and then examined how well they performed on exam questions that measured critical and analytical thinking. They found that students performed better on these questions following interteaching sessions.

In addition to studies examining the relative efficacy of interteaching, researchers have begun to examine which of interteaching's several components make it effective (Cannella-Malone and others, 2009; Saville, Cox, O'Brien, and Vanderveldt, 2011; Saville and Zinn, 2009) along with ways to increase its efficacy (Goto and Schneider, 2010; Lambert and Saville, 2012). In short, the growing body of research suggests that interteaching may be an effective and enjoyable alternative to more traditional teaching methods, offering a viable model to foster a total-classroom learning community.

Team-Based Learning

Whereas interteaching, with its emphasis on continually changing discussion groups, creates more of a total-classroom learning community, other teaching methods create communities consisting of smaller, more stable teams. Consequently, these teaching methods are nice examples of within-classroom learning communities. One such method is team-based learning (TBL), which is an instructional method that focuses on students' abilities to apply course content in structured teams throughout the semester

(Michaelsen, Knight, and Fink, 2004). Teachers typically create heterogeneous teams of five to seven students based on factors that are most important for their particular courses. These factors might include students' major, class standing, gender, grades in relevant courses, anxiety about the course material, and previous exposure to course material. Students meet their teams during the first or second day of the course and remain in the same team for the semester (Michaelsen and others, 2004).

In a typical TBL course, teachers package the course content into six to eight modules. For each module, students participate in the following sequence of events (Michaelsen and others, 2004). First, students complete assigned readings outside of class with the help of a reading guide provided by the teacher. The reading guide helps students identify the most important concepts from the readings; it also helps them acquire the basic background knowledge they need to complete application activities in class. Next, students take an in-class individual quiz that covers the content presented in the readings to ensure that they understand the key concepts for the module. Once all students have completed the individual quiz, they get together and take the same quiz with their teammates. Teams then have a chance to appeal and provide rationale for any questions they missed. If the appeal is accepted, the team members earn back points for that particular question. Finally, teams can request that the teacher provide a short lecture on any concepts that are still unclear. This sequence of events typically happens during one class period, at the end of which students have been exposed to the course material in four different formats (that is, individual reading, quizzes, appeals, and lecture).

During subsequent class periods that cover a particular module, students work in their teams to complete application activities. Application activities require students to integrate the information from the readings and should be challenging enough to generate discussion. All teams should receive the same problem or scenario in which they have to make a specific decision (for example, suppose your team is putting together a campaign to educate the public about the impact of drugs on a developing fetus and you could focus on only one. Which of the following would you focus on and why?: alcohol, cigarettes, marijuana, cocaine). Because teams remain intact for the duration of the semester (which means that individual contributions are identifiable; Brickner, Harkins, and Ostrom, 1986) and because the application activities are challenging, there is a reduction in social loafing (a phenomenon in which individuals show less total effort when they are members of a group; see Harkins and Petty, 1982). Once teams have spent some time discussing the application problems, they come to a decision about how they would attempt to solve the issue. Because the teammates must come to an agreement about their decision, team discussion tends to be productive. Once each team has come to a decision, they simultaneously report their decision, usually by holding up a sign that denotes a particular answer or by entering their answers electronically (for example, using clickers). The key is that the teams report their answers at the same time, which ensures they do not change their decision as they hear other teams' explanations. The simultaneous reporting of decisions often leads to a productive whole-class discussion, because not all teams make the same decision.

Another key feature of TBL is the grading system. Students' grades are composed of an individual component, which is made up of individual assignments, quizzes, and exams, and a team component, which is made up of team quizzes and activities. Peer evaluations, which ensure that students contribute to the team, also make up part of the team grade. Peer evaluations hold students accountable to each other because students need to be prepared for team quizzes and activities.

TBL is a flexible teaching method. For example, it can be used in large classes (Michaelsen, 2002) but must be executed with more precision than in smaller classes where classroom management is simpler. In classrooms with fixed seating, teachers can designate certain spaces in the room for each team. Team members then must figure out in what configuration they should sit so they can hear each other. TBL tends to fit best in classes that last at least seventy-five minutes, but it is possible to conduct TBL in fifty-minute class periods. If teachers feel that fifty minutes is not enough time, students can complete the individual quizzes on-line before they come to class. That way, class time can be saved for the team quiz, the appeals process, and the mini-lecture. Teachers may also need to be more creative in designing application activities that can be completed in fifty minutes, or they may have to design activities that take more than one class period to complete.

One of the authors has used TBL in a developmental psychology course, a lifespan human development course, and a women and gender course, with class sizes ranging from five to seventy students. TBL has also been used in Introductory Psychology (Marrs, 2011), Industrial–Organizational Psychology (Haberyan, 2007), Introductory Biology (Carmichael, 2009), and medical school courses (for example, Chung and others, 2009; Hunt and others, 2003; Zgheib and others, 2010).

Research. TBL has been used across many disciplines, and studies have shown that TBL tends to produce numerous positive outcomes. For example, Kelly and others (2005) found that TBL produced more learner-to-learner and less learner-to-instructor engagement than lecture-based teaching methods. Other studies have found that TBL improves overall performance (Carmichael, 2009; Haberyan, 2007; Tsay and Brady, 2010; Zgheib, Simaan, and Sabra, 2010) and problem solving (Chung, Rhee, Baik, and A, 2009). Although these studies provide but a sample of the research on TBL, they demonstrate that TBL—which contains elements of both total- and within-classroom learning communities—seems to be effective at increasing student engagement as well as student interaction.

Cooperative Learning in Large, Lecture-Based Courses

Interteaching and TBL are instructional techniques that sometimes require substantial course revision (for example, Boyce and Hineline, 2002; Michaelsen and others, 2004). Teachers who want to create learning communities in their classrooms, but who do not want to revamp their courses completely, can blend cooperative learning with more traditional teaching techniques (for example, lecture).

Lenning and Ebers (1999) argued that within-class learning communities must be cooperative in nature. Two essential components of cooperative learning groups are positive interdependence and individual accountability (Johnson and Johnson, 1999). Positive interdependence can be achieved in lecture-based courses by having students submit group assignments for which everyone receives the same grade; teachers can also create positive interdependence by giving students extra credit when every member of a group scores above a specified criterion on individual tests or by making part of each student's course grade dependent on the performance of other group members (which can also be incorporated in interteaching courses; see Boyce and Hineline, 2002; Saville and Zinn, 2009). Ultimately, when students in a lecture-based course depend on others for learning and for part of their course grade, they tend to become as concerned with others' performance as they are with their own.

The second characteristic of cooperative learning groups is individual accountability. Students must feel that they are responsible for their contributions to the group. When their contributions are neither identified nor evaluated, students are more likely to engage in social loafing (Karau and Williams, 1993). Thus, individual accountability is more likely in lecture-based courses when the group size is small (and members cannot hide in the crowd) and group members take their own tests. Another way to ensure individual accountability is to randomly call on students to answer for their group. In Kagan's (1994) numbered heads together technique, each group member is given a number (from one to the maximum number in each group). Group members put their "heads together" to solve a problem or answer a question. The instructor then randomly picks a number to determine which student will share the group's answer. If the instructor picks the number two, for example, then all students holding that number must answer for their group.

Although there are numerous more formal cooperative-learning strategies described in the literature (for example, the jigsaw classroom, see Aronson and Patnoe, 1997; group investigation, see Sharan and Sharan, 1992), it is not necessary to adopt one of these strategies. Rather, teachers can structure cooperative learning to fit their own goals, teaching style, and classes. One of us creates cooperative learning communities of four students in her large lecture-based courses. These groups get together every other class period to complete a cooperative learning activity (for example, designing an experiment or solving a complex problem). Every member of the group receives the same grade (which is similar to aspects of TBL). Other times, members of these groups engage in smaller pair discussions (which is more like interteaching). Some cooperative learning experts argue that teachers should frequently change the groups so students get a chance to work with every other student in the class (Johnson and Johnson, 1999) to help promote a total-classroom learning community. This strategy, however, may be impractical in large college classrooms. Frequent switching may also prevent groups from developing cohesiveness, which takes time to grow (Tuckman, 1965).

Research. There has been a great deal of research on cooperative learning in college settings, and summarizing that literature is beyond the scope of this chapter. In general, though, the results of this research have shown that, in addition to promoting academic achievement, cooperative learning increases liking among students, perceived social support from peers and instructors, and positive attitudes toward college (see Johnson, Johnson, and Smith, 1998; Springer, Stanne, and Donovan, 1999). These outcomes help build small communities of learners, even in larger, lecture-based courses.

Lessons Learned and Recommendations

Each of the aforementioned teaching strategies capitalizes on cooperative learning by requiring that students work together to enhance the learning of everyone involved. Anecdotal and empirical evidence support the implementation of interteaching, team-based learning, and more informal cooperative learning strategies in college classrooms. Nevertheless, teachers wishing to use these methods to create classroom-based learning communities and to improve student performance should be aware of two primary pitfalls they may encounter, both of which may occur when initially introducing these methods and later on down the line. First, we have found that students are sometimes initially resistant to "alternative" teaching methods, especially when they have learned how to be successful in more traditionally taught courses (for example, getting a high grade). Some students might ask, "Why are you making us do this when we already know how to get good grades?" Of course, "good grades" may or may not be a valid measure of learning, but for better or for worse (probably for worse), good grades are all that matter to some students (for example, Walvoord and Anderson, 2010). Fortunately, alternative teaching methods often produce increases in student-learning outcomes (for example, exam scores) and in long-term retention. Thus, it is important from the start that you explain to students why you are using these methods, what outcomes are likely to result if they do what you ask, and that you have their best interest in mind.

Second, when using any teaching strategy that places students into groups, one must be aware of common problems that frequently arise. Arguably the biggest problem when using groups is social loafing. Social loafing can promote free riding, where some members decrease their contributions assuming others will pick up the slack (Kerr and Bruun, 1983), and the sucker effect, where group members who perceive others as free riders reduce their own effort to avoid being taken advantage of—which, if all members behave similarly, will likely reduce overall group output (Kerr, 1983). A second problem revolves around personality differences, where group members simply do not get along with one another and thus perform ineffectively. A third problem entails having one (or a few) group member(s) dominate the others, which can produce subpar performance, depending on how the other group members respond to the dominant individual(s). Finally, student absenteeism may be an outcome of using group-based teaching methods (possibly as a side effect of the first three problems).

One way to alleviate social loafing (and its associated problems) is to create individual accountability. Fortunately, each of the methods we described has mechanisms for identifying the contributions of individual students. Interteaching, with its emphasis on pair discussions, makes it difficult for students to loaf—by definition, a pair *discussion* requires the input of two people. In addition, students report how well their discussions went, along with reasons why they went well or poorly (for example, "My partner had not completed her prep guide"), which introduces individual accountability. TBL increases individual accountability by including team quizzes and peer evaluations. Because the peer evaluations ask group members to rate one another's contributions, students are more likely to come prepared and contribute to the group. Finally, as noted previously, two possible ways to increase accountability when using cooperative learning in larger, lecture-based courses are to have students form smaller groups (so students cannot "hide") and to use a method where one member of a group must speak for the rest. In short, addressing each of these problems up front and early will likely create a better environment in which students can enjoy and benefit from their learning community experience.

With regard to personality differences and dominant students, it is important to remind students that getting along with others and working cooperatively are skills that will likely benefit them throughout their lives. Thus, it is in their best interest to work together to achieve collective success (for example, McKeachie and Svinicki, 2006). Although these issues may be a bit trickier to address than social loafing, it is nevertheless important to take steps to ensure that personality differences and dominant students do not have a negative impact on the learning communities that are being created. Finally, there are many ways to reduce absenteeism, not the least of which include periodically taking attendance (for example, Shimoff and Catania, 2001), making supplemental course materials dependent on attendance (for example, Hove and Corcoran, 2008), including a small number of attendance points as part of each student's course grade (for example, Boyce and Hineline, 2002), and using peer evaluations (Cestone, Levin, and Lane, 2008).

Conclusion

Although the search for effective teaching methods is likely as old as formal education itself, the recent emergence of learning communities—and more specifically, classroom-based learning communities—provides another way in which teachers can capitalize on what is known about college-student success. Interteaching, team-based learning, and cooperative learning in lecture-based classrooms are three teaching strategies that differ in form but capitalize on cooperative learning. Teachers interested in creating learning communities in their classrooms might wish to consider these methods as effective and enjoyable alternatives to the more-traditional teaching methods that tend to dominate in higher education.

References

Aronson, E., and Patnoe, S. *The Jigsaw Classroom: Building Cooperation in the Classroom.* (2nd ed.). New York: Addison Wesley Longman, 1997.

Astin, A. W. "The Impact of Dormitory Living on Students." *Educational Record*, 1973, *54*, 204–210.

Astin, A. W. "Student Involvement: A Developmental Theory for Higher Education." *Journal of College Student Personnel*, 1999, *40*, 518–529. (Reprinted from *Journal of College Student Development*, 1984, 25, 297–308).

Astin, A. W. *What Matters in College?: Four Critical Years Revisited.* San Francisco: Jossey-Bass, 1993.

Bielaczyc, K., and Collins, A. "Learning Communities in Classrooms: A Reconceptualization of Educational Practice." In C. M. Reigeluth (ed.), *Instructional-Design Theories and Models: A New Paradigm of Instructional Theory* (pp. 269–292). Mahwah, N.J.: Lawrence Erlbaum Associates, 1999.

Boyce, T. E., and Hineline, P. N. "Interteaching: A Strategy for Enhancing the User-Friendliness of Behavioral Arrangements in the College Classroom." *The Behavior Analyst*, 2002, *25*, 215–226.

Brickner, M. A., Harkins, S. G., and Ostrom, T. M. "Effects of Personal Involvement: Thought-Provoking Implications of Social Loafing." *Journal of Personality and Social Psychology*, 1986, *51*, 763–769.

Cannella-Malone, H. I., Axe, J. B., and Parker, E. D. "Interteach Preparation: A Comparison of the Effects of Answering Versus Generating Study Guide Questions on Quiz Scores." *Journal of the Scholarship of Teaching and Learning*, 2009, *9*, 22–35.

Carmichael, J. "Team-Based Learning Enhances Performance in Introductory Biology." *Journal of College Science Teaching*, 2009, *38*, 54–61.

Cestone, C. M., Levin, R. E., and Lane, D. R. "Peer Assessment and Evaluation in Team-Based Learning." In L. K. Michaelsen, M. Sweet, and D. X. Parmelee (eds.), *Team-Based Learning: Small Group Learning's Next Big Step* (pp. 69–78). New Directions for Teaching and Learning, no. 116. San Francisco: Jossey-Bass, 2008.

Chickering, A. W. *Education and Identity.* San Francisco: Jossey-Bass, 1969.

Chung, E., Rhee, J., Baik, Y., and A, O. "The Effect of Team-Based Learning in Medical Ethics Education." *Medical Teacher*, 2009, *31*, 1013–1017.

Connor-Greene, P. A. "Problem-Based Learning." In W. Buskist and S. F. Davis (eds.), *The Handbook of the Teaching of Psychology* (pp. 70–77). Malden, Mass.: Blackwell, 2005.

Duch, B. J., Groh, S. E., and Allen, D. E. (eds.). *The Power of Problem-Based Learning: A Practical "How to" for Teaching Undergraduate Courses in Any Discipline*. Sterling, Va.: Stylus, 2001.

Emurian, H. H., and Zheng, P. "Programmed Instruction and Interteaching Applications to Teaching Java™: A Systematic Replication." *Computers in Human Behavior*, 2010, *26*, 1166–1175.

Gamson, Z. F. "The Origins of Contemporary Learning Communities: Residential Colleges, Experimental Colleges, and Living-Learning Communities." In D. Dezure (ed.), *Learning from Change* (pp. 113–116). Washington, D.C.: American Association for Higher Education and Sterling, Va.: Stylus Publishing, 2000.

Goto, K., and Schneider, J. "Learning through Teaching: Challenges and Opportunities in Facilitating Student Learning in Food Science and Nutrition by Using the Interteaching Approach." *Journal of Food Science Education*, 2010, *9*, 31–35.

Haberyan, A. "Team-Based Learning in an Industrial/Organizational Psychology Course." *North American Journal of Psychology*, 2007, *9*, 143–152.

Harkins, S. G., and Petty, R. E. "Effects of Task Difficulty and Task Uniqueness on Social Loafing." *Journal of Personality and Social Psychology*, 1982, *43*, 1214–1229.

Hove, M. C., and Corcoran, K. J. "If You Post It Will They Come? Lecture Availability in Introductory Psychology." *Teaching of Psychology*, 2008, *35*, 91–95.

Hunt, D. P., Haidet, P., Coverdale, J. H., and Richards, B. "The Effect of Using Team Learning in an Evidence-Based Medicine Course for Medical Students." *Teaching and Learning in Medicine*, 2003, *15*, 131–139.

Johnson, D. W., and Johnson, R. T. *Learning Together and Alone: Cooperative, Competitive, and Individualistic Learning*. Boston: Allyn and Bacon, 1999.

Johnson, D. W., Johnson, R. T., and Smith, K. A. "Cooperative Learning Returns to College: What Evidence Is There That It Works?" *Change*, 1998, *30*(4), 26–35.

Kagan, S. *Cooperative Learning*. San Clemente, Calif.: Kagan, 1994.

Karau, S. J., and Williams, K. D. "Social Loafing: A Meta-Analytic Review and Theoretical Integration." *Journal of Personality and Social Psychology*, 1993, *65*, 681–706.

Kelly, P. A., and others. "A Comparison of In-Class Learner Engagement across Lecture, Problem-Based Learning, and Team Learning Using the STROBE Classroom Observation Tool." *Teaching and Learning in Medicine*, 2005, *17*, 112–118.

Kerr, N. L. "Motivation Losses in Small Groups: A Social Dilemma Analysis." *Journal of Personality and Social Psychology*, 1983, *45*, 819–828.

Kerr, N. L., and Bruun, S. E. "The Dispensability of Member Effort and Group Motivation Losses: Free-Rider Effects." *Journal of Personality and Social Psychology*, 1983, *44*, 78–94.

Kuh, G. D. "Assessing What Really Matters to Student Learning: Inside the National Survey of Student Engagement." *Change*, 2001, *33*(3), 10–17.

Lambert, T., and Saville, B. K. "Interteaching and the Testing Effect: A Preliminary Analysis." *Teaching of Psychology*, 2012, *39*, 194–198.

Lenning, O. T., and Ebbers, L. H. *The Powerful Potential of Learning Communities: Improving Education for the Future*. ASHE-ERIC Higher Education Report, Vol. 26, No. 6. Washington, D.C.: Graduate School of Education and Human Development, George Washington University, 1999.

Marrs, H. "Increasing Learner Engagement with Team-Based Learning." In R. L. Miller, and others (eds.), *Promoting Student Engagement, Vol. 1: Programs, Techniques and Opportunities* (pp. 185–191). Washington, D.C.: Society for Teaching Psychology, 2011.

McKeachie, W. J., and Svinicki, M. *McKeachie's Teaching Tips: Strategies, Research, and Theory for College and University Teachers.* (12th ed.). Boston: Houghton Mifflin, 2006.

Michaelsen, L. K. "Team-Based Learning in Large Classes." In C. Stanley and E. Porter (eds.), *Engaging Large Classes: Strategies and Techniques for College Faculty* (pp. 67–83). New York: Anker, 2002.

Michaelsen, L. K., Knight, A. B., and Fink, L. *Team-Based Learning: A Transformative Use of Small Groups in College Teaching.* Sterling, Va.: Stylus Publishing, 2004.

Pascarella, E. T., and Terenzini, P. *How College Affects Students: Findings and Insights from Twenty Years of Research.* San Francisco: Jossey-Bass, 1991.

Saville, B. K., Cox, T., O'Brien, S., Vanderveldt, A. "Interteaching: The Impact of Lectures on Student Performance." *Journal of Applied Behavior Analysis,* 2011, *44,* 937–941.

Saville, B. K., Lambert, T., and Robertson, S. "Interteaching: Bringing Behavioral Education into the 21st Century." *The Psychological Record,* 2011, *61,* 153–166.

Saville, B. K., and Zinn, T. E. "Interteaching: The Effects of Quality Points on Exam Scores." *Journal of Applied Behavior Analysis,* 2009, *42,* 369–374.

Saville, B. K., Zinn, T. E., and Elliott, M. P. "Interteaching versus Traditional Methods of Instruction: A Preliminary Analysis." *Teaching of Psychology,* 2005, *32,* 161–163.

Saville, B. K., and others. "A Comparison of Interteaching and Lecture in the College Classroom." *Journal of Applied Behavior Analysis,* 2006, *39,* 49–61.

Saville, B. K., and others. "Teaching Critical Thinking in Statistics and Research Methods." In D. S. Dunn, J. S. Halonen, and R. A. Smith (eds.), *Teaching Critical Thinking in Psychology: A Handbook of Best Practices* (pp. 149–160). Malden, Mass.: Wiley-Blackwell, 2008.

Scoboria, A., and Pascual-Leone, A. "An 'Interteaching' Informed Approach to Instructing Large Undergraduate Classes." *Journal of the Scholarship of Teaching and Learning,* 2009, *9,* 29–37.

Shapiro, N. S., and Levine, J. H. *Creating Learning Communities.* San Francisco: Jossey-Bass, 1999.

Sharan, Y., and Sharan, S. *Expanding Cooperative Learning through Group Investigation.* New York: Teachers College Press, 1992.

Shimoff, E., and Catania, A. C. "Effects of Recording Attendance on Grades in Introductory Psychology." *Teaching of Psychology,* 2001, *28,* 192–195.

Springer, L., Stanne, M. E., and Donovan, S. S. "Effects of Small-Group Learning on Undergraduates in Science, Mathematics, Engineering, and Technology: A Meta-Analysis." *Review of Educational Research,* 1999, *69,* 21–51.

Tsay, M., and Brady, M. "A Case Study of Cooperative Learning and Communication Pedagogy: Does Working in Teams Make a Difference?" *Journal of the Scholarship of Teaching and Learning,* 2010, *10,* 78–89.

Tsui, M. "Interteaching: Students as Teachers in Lower-Division Sociology Courses." *Teaching Sociology,* 2010, *38,* 28–34.

Tuckman, B. W. "Developmental Sequences in Small Groups." *Psychological Bulletin,* 1965, *63,* 384–399.

Walvoord, B. E., and Anderson, V. J. *Effective Grading: A Tool for Learning and Assessment in College.* (2nd ed.). San Francisco: Jossey-Bass, 2010.

Zeller, B. E. "We Learned So Much When You Weren't There!: Reflections on the Interteach Method and the Acephalous Classroom." *Teaching Theology and Religion,* 2010, *13,* 270–271.

Zgheib, N. K., Simaan, J. A., and Sabra, R. "Using Team-Based Learning to Teach Pharmacology to Second Year Medical Students Improves Student Performance." *Medical Teacher,* 2010, *32,* 130–136.

Zhao, C., and Kuh, G. D. "Adding Value: Learning Communities and Student Engagement." *Research in Higher Education,* 2004, *45,* 115–138.

BRYAN K. SAVILLE is an associate professor in the Department of Psychology at James Madison University.

NATALIE KERR LAWRENCE is an associate professor in the Department of Psychology at James Madison University.

KRISZTINA V. JAKOBSEN is an assistant professor in the Department of Psychology at James Madison University

NEW DIRECTIONS FOR TEACHING AND LEARNING • DOI: 10.1002/tl

6

Student-based organizations offer another approach to promote learning communities above and beyond particular curricular or classroom approaches. Not only can they create connections among students with shared disciplinary or professional interests on a single campus, but they also offer the possibility for creating connections to larger communities beyond an institution.

Using Student-Based Organizations Within a Discipline as a Vehicle to Create Learning Communities

Michael D. Hall

At first glance, the title of this chapter might appear to some readers as a bit of a contradiction in terms of juxtaposing "student-based organizations" and "learning communities." It certainly could be argued that student organizations do not meet more traditional definitions of learning communities, such as that provided by Smith, MacGregor, Matthews, and Gabelnick (2004) and cited in Chapter One. Traditional definitions of learning communities are firmly based in the curriculum, whereas student-based organizations typically represent cocurricular activities.

However, this volume has intentionally adopted a broad view of learning communities as any "intentionally developed community that will promote and maximize learning" (Lenning and Ebbers, 1999, p. 10), which clearly allows for the inclusion of a variety of learning community structures both within and across disciplines, including student-based organizations. In fact, Lenning and Ebbers's typology of learning communities defines "student learning communities" as "relatively small groups of students (and faculty) working together to enhance students' learning and to help students become well-rounded, broad-based individuals" (p. 15). Furthermore, there are growing indications of the benefits of fostering student engagement through experiences that are common to student organizations, such as shared learning experiences across students and increased informal student–faculty interaction (Guenther and Miller, 2011). The high

New Directions for Teaching and Learning, no. 132, Winter 2012 © Wiley Periodicals, Inc.
Published online in Wiley Online Library (wileyonlinelibrary.com) • DOI: 10.1002/tl.20037

levels of student engagement that can occur in student-based organizations also has been associated with increased academic retention and success, as well as with demonstrated competence in one's discipline (see Miller and Butler, 2011).

Student-based organizations routinely facilitate academic and social engagement while pursuing a variety of activities. For example, student-based organizations are frequently involved in community service, permit the development of student leadership abilities (for example, by serving as an officer or heading a committee), and provide valuable exposure to career information that may potentially enhance students' development of professional identity. This facilitation has been argued to be instrumental in student retention and success (for example, see Handelsman, Briggs, Sullivan, and Towler, 2005; Thielen, Stuber, Grover, and Weaver, 2011). When taken in conjunction with claims that peer groups represent the strongest influence on undergraduates (Astin, 1993), it effectively can be argued that student-based organizations offer powerful mechanisms to enhance student learning within a discipline. Thus, although student-based organizations differ from traditional conceptions of learning communities, they certainly meet the most critical aspects of any general definition of learning community by promoting learning within a student group and appear to be quite effective at reinforcing and extending what students learn within their courses.

This chapter attempts to summarize the benefits and basic challenges posed by student-based learning communities. It then provides a few general suggestions as to how to best address these challenges within student-based organizations. Challenges and recommendations are highlighted using relevant findings from the literature, as well as documented and anecdotal examples from an in-depth case study of a student-based honor society in psychology that I have coordinated at the local, regional, and international levels.

Examples of Student-Based Learning Communities

An appreciation for the relevance of developing best practices for student-based organizations can be gained from understanding just how pervasive these communities are. For example, the psychology program at James Madison University (JMU) where I work has several types of student-based organizations, each serving a different subset of students. Some student-based organizations at JMU are more inclusive, with open membership policies; others, such as honor societies and some departmentally sponsored groups, are more exclusive, with competition for membership. JMU's Psychology Club is open to all psychology students and provides an assortment of career-related events (for example, a series of invited presentations) and social activities for its members. JMU also has a chapter of the Association of Black Psychologists (ABPsi), which focuses on the professional development and support of Black psychologists, as well as addressing psychological issues within the Black community. Students have also formed peer groups with open membership in order to target particular societal issues. For example, members of JMU's chapter of Active Minds seek to raise awareness and promote education about the stigma associated with mental illness, and Psychologists for Sustainability promote education and activism about environmental stewardship. Additionally, a dedicated group of junior and senior psychology majors who are selected to serve as psychology peer advisors staff a peer advising and resource office in the psychology building for any student on campus to drop in to learn more about the psychology major or to obtain career-related information about psychology.

My relevant experience with student-based learning communities is with Psi Chi, the international honor society in psychology. As with most discipline-specific honor societies, membership in Psi Chi is by invitation and is limited to students who have exhibited outstanding academic performance both within the major and overall at the university. I began as a chapter advisor early in my career at my previous institution, and then served as a regional vice president. At JMU, I have continued to work as a chapter advisor, and most recently, served as the international president for the entire organization. Psi Chi represents one of the most common psychology-specific student organizations on campuses, and is likely the largest student organization within the discipline, with around 600,000 lifetime members. Furthermore, honor societies like Psi Chi encourage student engagement by providing frequent interactions between students and faculty, as well as leadership mentoring opportunities (Skinner and Belmont, 1993). Involvement in psychology-specific activities, including Psi Chi, has been shown to be positively correlated with student satisfaction with their major, as well as with grade point average (Strapp and Farr, 2010).

Psi Chi's purpose is "to encourage, stimulate, and maintain excellence in scholarship of the individual members in all fields, particularly in psychology, and to advance the science of psychology" (Psi Chi, n.d., para, 1; see www.psichi.org/About/purpose.aspx). The organization serves this purpose in a number of ways. First, it maintains an active presence in programming at regional and national conferences. At regional meetings, for example, there are opportunities for community building not only through sponsoring distinguished lectures from renowned researchers, but also social exchange and award events where local chapters from different areas can come together to share ideas and network. The organization also frequently maintains hospitality suites at regional conferences, where students can come to meet like-minded students from other areas as well as to meet with Psi Chi board members and regional representation to discuss career development and long-term interests for the organization. Student members receive access to a quarterly magazine (*Eye on Psi Chi*) containing a variety of useful career-related information (for example, how to success-fully apply to graduate programs) as well as the organization's own research journal that publishes original student research (*Psi Chi Journal of Under-graduate Research*). Members also qualify for a growing number of financial award programs for research and teaching-learning experiences across aca-demic levels (undergraduate, graduate, and faculty). At the local level, Psi Chi chapters are generally active in sponsoring career-relevant events on their campuses, such as hosting conferences and research symposia, arrang-ing for invited speakers from a host of subdisciplines in psychology, fund-raising to support student travel or departmental activities and awards, and typically are consistently involved in community service.

Given the frequency of its presence in psychology departments (with over 1,100 chapters in the United States and internationally), combined with its role in facilitating student engagement, Psi Chi can be considered a particularly effective model for a student-based learning community in psychology. Furthermore, the fact that similar honor societies are common-place across disciplines means that issues that apply to Psi Chi's operation are likely to be similarly encountered in other fields. Psi Chi also happens to be the student-based learning community with which I am most familiar. In light of these considerations I rely heavily on examples from Psi Chi (including personal anecdotes as well as examples from the organization's *Eye on Psi Chi* magazine, which is readily available on-line at http://www.psichi.org/pubs/eye/) to highlight common challenges and suggestions for best practices. My intention is for readers to find similarities with other student organizations centered in their own discipline or department that allow for useful generalizations that can inform their own work and guide their own practice.

Common Challenges Facing Student-Based Learning Communities

First, some of the difficulties for student-based learning communities that are most likely to be mentioned by students and faculty alike (and that are sometimes echoed in publications) will be listed and discussed. This list is not intended to be exhaustive nor are the challenges provided in any par-ticular order. Rather, the combination of challenges that are the most salient for a given organization tend to be unique to that institution, and more specifically, to that group of student and faculty members.

Time Constraints. One of the most common obstacles to both stu-dent and faculty engagement in student organizations is a lack of time to devote to organization activities. For example, students at JMU, like those in many other institutions, tend to have a high level of activism, and as a result, often retain active membership in several organizations simultane-ously. This kind of competition from other organizations has been previ-ously noted as a general challenge for Psi Chi members (Shaikh and

Camparo, 2009). In addition, our students frequently carry course loads with credit hours well beyond those required for full-time status. These factors, not to mention possible employment, tend to place very tight constraints on the time that students have available to devote to any student-based learning community. It also is noteworthy that this challenge is not limited to students. A lack of available time to devote to the organization also was identified as a major challenge in a recent national survey of Psi Chi faculty advisors (Domenech Rodríguez and McDougal, 2008).

Student organizations also typically have an inconsistent meeting schedule when compared to typical coursework, and these meetings are usually held after business hours so as not to conflict with student course schedules. For instance, our chapter of Psi Chi at JMU has recently been meeting around the dinner hour every other week. Although less frequent club meetings could make it more likely that students would be consistently available to participate, the absence of frequently scheduled meetings relative to traditional coursework may actually contribute to increased forgetfulness about upcoming events. In addition, later meeting times could present real problems for students who work at night or have a long driving commute to school.

Misperceptions about the Organization's Purpose. Another common barrier to student engagement within organizations is a frequent lack of awareness about the nature of the group and its utility. For example, many qualified students choose not to join Psi Chi because they view it as simply an honor society devoid of any sense of community. They often do not see membership as a beneficial way to connect to other like-minded students and faculty within the discipline, but rather simply regard it as another indicator of strong academic performance for their resume. I have even heard that some students regard membership as an excuse to generate money for the organization's use. They do not immediately recognize that the modest, one-time cost of their lifetime membership qualifies them for several awards that may help their career advancement, nor do they consider the fact that they will be put in touch with a lot of useful career-related information that can help them be better informed and prepared for the future. This perspective can particularly affect students with lower socioeconomic status, as they are likely unable and unwilling to pay joining fees when they are unaware of the direct benefits of membership. As a result, in some organizations this issue might even constitute a contributing factor to the underrepresentation of particular student groups, including ethnic minorities.

In Psi Chi this problem has become apparent in numerous ways within individual chapters, some of which were listed in a recent editorial column in the *Eye on Psi Chi* (Hall, 2011).In fact, a national survey of chapters identified the lack of knowledge about Psi Chi to be one of the most common reasons for students not joining (Spencer, Reyes, Sheel, and McFarland, 2001).

These kinds of issues also have been observed at regional and national levels. For example, even among students who do become members, there is still a percentage who do so presumably just to obtain another mark of excellence upon their transcript. Faculty advisors have frequently mentioned this to me at regional meetings, indicating that several students each term attend induction ceremonies only to never attend another meeting of the chapter. In Psi Chi this is noteworthy as the standard induction ceremony includes the new member reciting that they will regularly attend such meetings.

Psi Chi also has frequently had some student awards for a given year go unawarded for lack of a sufficient number of high-quality applications. This is not because high-caliber student research projects are lacking, as Psi Chi students are very well represented at regional and national meetings. Rather, in talking with many Psi Chi students at conferences, it appears that the students simply are not applying for the awards. There seems to be a general lack of awareness of award opportunities, particularly among graduate students, and when they do know about such awards, they tend to think that they are unlikely to be sufficiently competitive (for example, they overestimate the number of students applying for awards).

Lack of Personal Investment and Inclusiveness. It is a common phenomenon within student organizations to have the bulk of the work done by a dedicated few, usually chapter officers. Psi Chi faculty advisors have frequently told me of this occurring in their home chapters, mainly due to insufficient motivation from other members to get involved. In fact, it is not unusual to see all activities planned and coordinated by a single officer. I also have observed committee and event planning at chapter meetings where membership seems generally supportive of an idea until they are asked to volunteer their time. In other words, whereas Psi Chi officers are usually invested in the optimal functioning and growth of the organization, most members do not reflect similar levels of engagement in helping to meet the goals of the group.

A related, recurring issue is that student organizations continue to work independently rather than connecting with other groups on or off campus that have similar interests. In so doing, these groups miss an opportunity to expand the number of participating students in club events and thus to significantly expand club programming. Much of this exclusivity stems from how the group is initially defined. This is particularly true of honor societies, where there can be a sense of elitism associated with the group as a result of the academic requirements for membership. Often groups see themselves as an elite collective; by identifying with each other through their membership, they often are resistant to sharing information, responsibilities, and events with other like-minded groups. For example, I have had a relatively difficult time coordinating events across student clubs (for example, Psi Chi and Psychology Club) when mechanisms are not already in place to assist in coordinating activities (such as when both groups regularly meet together within a department). The organization might not even know whether it is appropriate to invite the involvement of other student organizations (as noted in Sleigh and Hall, 2011). Thus, part of the community building that occurs in these student organizations can actually pose a barrier to further growth and extension of that community.

Lack of Continuity. As the officers and seasoned members of the chapter graduate, there often is insufficient time to adequately transition new officers and members. As a result, I have often heard from faculty advisors that they might have an excellent year with students followed by a year where little gets accomplished. Becker (2010) even notes: "Experienced chapter advisors know that you can have good years, and you can have challenging years working with Psi Chi officer teams" and "the type of year a chapter has may be partly due to chance" (p. 22).

Recommendations for Developing Successful Student-Based Learning Communities

Before the reader becomes overwhelmed at the myriad obstacles facing student organizations, comfort should be taken in the fact that many of these obstacles can be overcome by faculty and student members consistently engaging in a few general practices. The inclusion of student members in these practices is deemed of critical importance, as peers have been previously cited to be the primary influence on the development of undergraduates (for example, Astin, 1993), and student organizations may be one of the most direct ways of exerting that influence in a career-relevant manner (for example, see Thielen and others, 2011).

Creating a Culture of Engagement. One of the simplest yet most effective recipes for success in student-based learning communities has to do with members collectively establishing a culture of expected engagement and accomplishment. Engagement can even be fostered by simply pointing out the limitations of passively being a member of the group, as is commonly discussed within honor society chapters (for example, revealing that most applicants to graduate programs also are honor society members, but relatively few of them are productive citizens within those societies). This practice can encourage personal involvement and accountability while helping to eliminate common misconceptions about the nature of the organization. As an extreme measure, departments also can schedule gaps during the business day so that student organizations can meet at more convenient times, thus revealing departmental commitment to those organizations while ensuring greater participation (as suggested by Thielen and others, 2011).

Early Marketing and Early Training of New Members. An obvious time for faculty advisors to contribute to the process of establishing a culture of engagement is when new members are joining the organization. For example, in our Psi Chi chapter I typically address incoming members at the beginning of their induction ceremony, emphasizing the importance and rewards of getting involved in the organization and their broader scientific communities. I have even found myself quoting the blockbuster film *Spiderman* in order to help get my message across (that is, "With great power comes great responsibility").

The utility of such an approach to encouraging active Psi Chi membership has been noted elsewhere, along with a host of other promotional strategies (see Shaikh and Camparo, 2009). These alternative strategies include discussing the organization and benefits of membership within classrooms, creating long-standing bulletin board displays, establishing a presence within departmental newsletters, and sponsoring department-wide events and awards. Engagement also can be promoted through department- or organization-driven orientation sessions, as well as through presentations delivered by existing members to introductory courses in the major.

Stress the Benefits and Value of Active Participation. Even if promotion increases attendance at events, additional steps are necessary to maximize active participation at those events. Students are often initially more willing to be involved if they can see how such involvement might directly benefit them, such as when service might lead to a line on a resume or vita. (This should not be surprising given the limited time that students typically have available for cocurricular activities). For example, student-based learning communities afford students valuable opportunities to acquire and practice leadership skills that will serve them well in their chosen profession, as Smith and O'Loughlin Brooks (2011) indicated for Psi Beta (the national honor society in psychology for community colleges).

Student organizations also can appeal to the individual interests of many students by offering a wide variety of programming and incentives. The Psi Chi chapters that I have been involved in have therefore tried to include an array of career-related informational events in psychology (for example, guest speakers representing a mixture of faculty in psychology and affiliated departments, along with professionals from the community), as well as fund-raising activities, departmental service, and community service. The inclusion of service activities is consistent with the suggested benefits of incorporating service learning components within student-based learning from Chapter One (Love, 2012). One example of such service by members of my Psi Chi chapter was when they recently organized the department's annual undergraduate research symposium. In so doing, participating members not only could indicate that service within their individual records but also gained insight into how to organize and deliver conference sessions. Similarly, Psi Chi as an organization has increased the number and size of research awards in exchange for student involvement in regional and national programming and organization-based publications.

Locally, student-based organizations can demonstrate a benefit of membership to students by ensuring consistent involvement of the faculty at meetings of the organization. A strong faculty presence helps students to become better acquainted with individual faculty members, which may foster potential future mentoring relationships. This can be particularly useful in large departments where there might otherwise be limited opportunity for individual interaction between students and professors. For example, throughout the year our local chapter of Psi Chi sponsors several invited talks by different faculty members about career development and their specific areas of research. These presentations tend to initiate further conversations with interested students and often lead to inquiry about potentially working in a faculty member's research laboratory. Students recognize that direct research experience can be an excellent source of recommendation letters for future applications for jobs and graduate study. In many cases, such research experience would not have been possible without the initial connections with faculty that were afforded by meetings of the organization.

Identify and Maintain Strong Leadership. Another effective way to avoid lapses in continuous student involvement and to strengthen the engagement of others is to identify and maintain strong faculty and student leadership that can inspire other members by consistently serving as examples of the benefits of service. Weaver (2008) identifies several fundamental ways to identify strong leaders for Psi Chi that apply equally well to other student organizations. Primary among these is paying attention to who is consistently showing up for club activities, as this represents a clear demonstration of enthusiasm for and commitment to the group, as well as being open to possible future service in it. Also recommended is permitting existing officers to identify additional nominees for officer positions based upon recognition of the greatest contributors to meetings and events throughout the year. Once elected, it also is critical to smoothly transition new leadership so that they can immediately perform well. Others (for example, Becker, 2010; adapted from Johnson and Johnson, 2009) have further highlighted the importance of officers sharing leadership while also retaining some individual tasks as a way to maximize effectiveness in their elected roles.

Distribute the Wealth. Although student officers are typically responsible for all event planning and execution, other members can become more personally invested in an organization by similarly imparting to them ownership of specific club activities. This could occur by increasing the number of officer positions (for example, JMU's Psi Chi chapter includes a membership coordinator, who helps process new member information and requests), as well as by assigning nonofficers as chairs for a variety of committees (for example, see Thielen and others, 2011). Ultimately, faculty members need to remind themselves that these are student-based organizations, and as a result, the more ideas that can be fostered and developed directly by students, the better the outcome in terms of participation.

Student-based organizations also can benefit tremendously by inviting the participation of other groups and/or coordinating activities with them. For example, involvement of other student-based learning communities can compensate for minimal involvement by particular members and thereby expand the effective size of the community. Certainly, the scope of planned service activities can grow whenever additional people are available to help with arrangement and execution of the events. Several benefits of inclusiveness across organizations were summarized for Psi Chi chapters in a recent *Eye on Psi Chi* article (Sleigh and Hall, 2011), including provision of better access to career information, improved recruitment of new members, fostering leadership development, and increasing the impact of service activities, particularly for small organizations.

Involving people outside the immediate learning community is as simple as identifying and contacting other local groups with similar interests. For instance, a student-based organization can sponsor department-wide events that would likely be of interest to other majors outside the group, such as hosting a colloquium series. There also is no reason why invitations need be limited to people within the given major. Rather, some events may concern interdisciplinary topics, and thus could prompt the invitation of another student-based organization on campus that has similar interests to aid in their organization. For example, my psychological research interests also tend to involve common speech and hearing research issues and thus would likely be of interest to budding speech scientists. Collaboration should even be possible with student-based organizations at other institutions. This is particularly true in locations where there are nearby institutions, as increased proximity would afford opportunity to share programming information with like-minded groups across campuses (for example, other Psi Chi chapters).

Getting the Word Out. Maximizing the involvement of student members requires vigilant communication. In modern institutions of learning, information is available for students in a variety of formats. These formats include traditional types of communication (for example, verbal announcements, posted or distributed flyers, newsletters and formal publications), as well as an array of electronic forms of communication (for example, e-mail messages, dedicated local and organization-wide websites, listservs, electronic bulletin boards, and social media alternatives, as detailed in Chapter Seven on virtual learning communities in psychology).

To be at their most effective, it is important for student organizations to be responsive to these alternatives and consider communicating with students in a variety of ways. Furthermore, it is important for organizations to recognize that not all forms of communication are equally effective across contexts. Rather, student-based learning communities should seek to rely most heavily on the means by which students most commonly choose to receive their information. For instance, two sets of observations necessitated recent discussions by Psi Chi's board of directors that led to the development of a societywide Facebook page. First, several individual chapters had already created Psi Chi Facebook pages as a method of information sharing. Second, individual students had indicated at regional conferences a frequent lack of awareness of e-mail messages that were sent by the organization. When taken together, these observations suggest that Psi Chi students might rely on information from social networking environments more heavily in some instances than on traditional e-mail.

Traditional forms of information sharing in student-based learning communities are generally unidirectional. In other words, information is sent to members without the possibility of a direct reply. However, a variety of bidirectional formats of communication also are available for use by student groups (for examples, see Chapter Seven). Many of these options (such as forum postings or on-line surveys) are asynchronous in that there is a delay imposed before the reply stemming from the fact that the recipient waits until a convenient time to view the sent message. This type of communication is useful for making announcements and collecting information from members over an extended period of at least a few days (as could be done in on-line voting).

Web-based synchronous forms of communication (such as chatrooms and Skype) represent even more powerful tools for student-based learning communities. They provide a means of reaching organization members who are located remotely (such as members who have a long commute and thus cannot stay on campus for late-night meetings), as well as other related groups (for example, chapters of the organization at other locations). For example, a U.S. Psi Chi chapter recently had a Skype discussion about starting and running a chapter with an interested group of psychology students in Guatemala. There also are chapters at institutions with a heavy on-line education component where there would be no learning community without the ability to conduct virtual meetings through synchronous communication methods. Thielen and others (2011) also revealed that such synchronous electronic communication could be facilitated by integrating it within existing on-line course delivery mechanisms. It is likely that, given the flexibility of participation offered by synchronous on-line communication, such approaches could soon become more and more commonplace within student-based learning communities. Furthermore, given the availability of synchronous on-line communication, it already is helping to extend connections between students beyond local groups to corresponding national and international communities.

There are other ways as well in which technology has helped put Psi Chi in a unique position as a student-based organization to be able to facilitate community-building both locally and globally. For instance, the fact that all members receive electronic access to both the *Eye on Psi Chi* magazine and more frequently occurring e-mail news digests means that all members are immediately put in touch with organizational event planning, including anticipated meetings of the Psi Chi community at regional and national conventions, as well as with career-relevant information for the discipline via upcoming lectures, award postings, and available articles.

All members also receive electronic access to the organization's journal, which is a general research-based publication. This publication was initially restricted to undergraduate first-author contributors but has recently been expanded to include reviewed submissions from any contributing members of the organization (that is, faculty, graduate students, and undergraduates). As a result, the journal is another powerful tool for integrating the Psi Chi community with the larger research community in psychology.

Finally, by being able to couple electronic communication across all international members with representation and programming at regional, national, and international conventions, Psi Chi also is in a position where it can establish a truly international network of young professionals in the discipline. In fact, Harold Takooshian, former Psi Chi president and former president of Division 52 of the American Psychological Association (International Psychology), has even indicated that because of its concentration on students, Psi Chi may be in a better position to serve this early networking role than larger professional organizations like the American Psychological Association. Certainly, not every student-based organization has the luxury of Psi Chi's size and growth potential. Thus, not every organization will be afforded the same opportunities for regional and international community building. However, Psi Chi provides many useful examples of ways in which connections can be made between students as well as faculty within a discipline, without being restricted by where members of the organization live and work. It also reveals a few ways in which student-based organizations can move beyond insular members-only groups to contribute to the larger disciplines with which they are associated.

Conclusion

In summary, student-based organizations should be recognized as a viable and important form of learning communities. They bring like-minded students together to spend more time engaged in career-relevant activities. In so doing, they represent a powerful additional source of career-relevant information and personal development for students, while also providing them with valuable hands-on leadership and service experience that augments what they can acquire within classroom settings. Furthermore, there is a proliferation of student organizations at every institution and within almost every discipline. They therefore warrant academic attention to determine how to help students get the most out of these formative experiences. For now, it is hoped that the suggestions contained in this chapter can contribute to developing a set of domain-general guidelines that could help bolster a variety of student-based learning communities across a variety of disciplines.

References

Astin, A. W. *What Matters in College: Four Critical Years Revisited*. San Francisco: Jossey-Bass, 1993.

Becker, S. E. "Building a Strong Officer Team." *Eye on Psi Chi*, 2010, *15*(1), 22–27.

Domenech Rodríguez, M. M., and McDougal, K. "Faculty Advisor's Voices: Chapter Growth Challenges in Leading Local Chapters." *Eye on Psi Chi*, 2008, *12*(4), 20–23.

Eye on Psi Chi, n.d. Retrieved December 12, 2011, from http://www.psichi.org/pubs /eye/.

Guenther, C., and Miller, R. L. "Factors That Promote Engagement." In R. L. Miller, and others (eds.), *Promoting Student Engagement. Vol. 1: Programs, Techniques and Opportunities*. Washington, D.C.: American Psychological Association, 2011.

Hall, M. D. "On the Consequences of Inaction." *Eye on Psi Chi*, 2011, *15*(2), 4.

Handelsman, M. M., Briggs, W. L., Sullivan, N., and Towler, A. "A Measure of College Student Course Engagement." *Journal of Education Research*, 2005, *98*, 184–191.

Johnson, D. W., and Johnson, F. P. *Joining Together: Group Theory and Group Skills*. (10th ed.). Columbus, Ohio: Pearson Publishing, 2009.

Lenning, O. T., and Ebbers, L. H. *The Powerful Potential of Learning Communities: Improving Education for the Future*. ASHE-ERIC Higher Education Report, Vol. 26, No. 6. Washington, D.C.: George Washington University, 1999.

Love, A. "The Growth and Current State of Learning Communities in Higher Education." In K. Buch & K. Barron (eds.), *Discipline-Centered Learning Communities: Creating Connections among Students and Faculty within a Major*. Washington, D.C.: American Psychological Association, 2012.

Miller, R. L., and Butler, J. M. "Outcomes Associated with Student Engagement." In R. L. Miller, and others (eds.), *Promoting Student Engagement. Vol. 1: Programs, Techniques and Opportunities*. Washington, D.C.: American Psychological Association, 2011.

Psi Chi. "Purpose & Mission Statements." n.d. Retrieved December 12, 2011, from www.psichi.org/About/purpose.aspx.

Shaikh, A., and Camparo, L. B. "Students Taking Charge: The Role of Psi Chi Chapters in Facilitating Learning." *Eye on Psi Chi*, 2009, *13*(2), 27–28.

Skinner, E. A., and Belmont, M. J. "Motivation in the Classroom: Reciprocal Effects of Teacher Behavior and Student Engagement Across the School Year." *Journal of Educational Psychology*, 1993, *85*, 571–581.

Sleigh, M. J., and Hall, M. D. "Collaboration: Why Our Exclusive Honor Society Should Be Inclusive." *Eye on Psi Chi*, 2011, *15*(2), 26–29.

Smith, B. L., MacGregor, J., Matthews, R. S., and Gabelnick, F. *Learning Communities: Reforming Undergraduate Education*. San Francisco: Jossey-Bass, 2004.

Smith, V. T., and O'Loughlin Brooks, J. L. "Psi Beta as an Avenue of Engagement." In R. L. Miller, and others (eds.), *Promoting Student Engagement. Vol. 1: Programs, Techniques and Opportunities*. Washington, D.C.: American Psychological Association, 2011.

Spencer, T. D., Reyes, C. J., Sheel, L., and McFarland, T. "Why Don't All Eligible Psychology Students Join Psi Chi?" *Psi Chi Journal of Undergraduate Research*, 2001, *6*(1), 37.

Strapp, C. M., and Farr, R. J. "To Get Involved or Not: The Relation Among Extracurricular Involvement, Satisfaction, and Academic Achievement." *Teaching of Psychology*, 2010, *37*(1), 50–54.

Thielen, K., Stuber, D., Grover, C., and Weaver, K. "Engaging Students Through Psychology Organizations." In R. L. Miller, and others (eds.), *Promoting Student Engagement. Vol. 1: Programs, Techniques and Opportunities*. Washington, D.C.: American Psychological Association, 2011.

Weaver, K. A. "Leadership Development and Strategies for Engaging Students." *Eye on Psi Chi*, 2008, *12*(3), 26–31.

MICHAEL D. HALL *is a professor in the Department of Psychology at James Madison University and a past-president of Psi Chi, the international honor society in psychology.*

NEW DIRECTIONS FOR TEACHING AND LEARNING • DOI: 10.1002/tl

7

Virtual learning communities (VLCs) provide a new vehicle for creating connections among stakeholders within academic disciplines and departments. This chapter describes the innovative use of information and computer technology (ICT) to create VLCs that can extend and enhance the impact of the traditional face-to-face learning communities described in preceding chapters.

Virtual Learning Communities Centered Within a Discipline: Future Directions

Anita L. Blanchard, James R. Cook

Over a decade ago, Lenning and Ebbers (1999) envisioned that ICT could be used to create VLCs as a "future" form of learning communities. Indeed, almost all academic departments—including psychology—depend heavily on the use of ICT to create and sustain connections among students, departments, and curricula. Similarly, most discipline-centered learning communities use ICT to enhance the impact of their communities and to facilitate the quantity and quality of interactions among community members. In this chapter, we discuss current technologies and the ways that they enable and promote intersections between virtual communities and other types of discipline-centered learning communities. We begin with a definition of VLCs, along with a description of the different ICTs that may be used in constructing VLCs. We then describe the expected benefits and challenges of discipline-centered VLCs, provide a hypothetical example of a discipline-centered VLC, and close with some advice on ways that academic departments can use technology to enhance student success.

Definition of Virtual Learning Communities

We define VLCs as groups of students, faculty, advisors, mentors, and teaching assistants who interact and connect with one another through an array of ICT systems. These communities can bridge across classes and across years in a program and may include former students or community

NEW DIRECTIONS FOR TEACHING AND LEARNING, no. 132, Winter 2012 © Wiley Periodicals, Inc.
Published online in Wiley Online Library (wileyonlinelibrary.com) • DOI: 10.1002/tl.20038

professionals who can serve as mentors or supervisors. The content of interactions can range from help with homework, advising information, departmental announcements, internship and postgraduate job opportunities and other topics that stimulate students' intellectual curiosity or facilitate bonding with their major and with one another.

In considering where VLCs fit in Lenning and Ebbers's (1999) typology of learning communities, VLCs can be a virtual extension of a traditional, face-to-face student, classroom, residential, or curriculum-centered LC. However, VLCs can also occur as separate and unique learning communities that may be offered instead of or alongside other forms of learning communities within an academic unit. This usually occurs in the context of on-line courses or other distance-learning efforts. For example, more and more departments are teaching on-line courses or other distance-learning programs. In either case, VLCs are designed to help students become part of a community of learners either when face-to-face interactions are not viable or to complement and extend the traditional interactions of an academic community.

Technological Components of VLCs

The central purpose of a VLC is to bring people together to provide support, exchange knowledge, and facilitate interactions and connections among members. The nature of the interactions and connections is determined in part by the ICT used to develop and support the VLC. For example, one important distinction is between synchronous (that is, real time) and asynchronous (that is, delayed) ICT. Synchronous ICT (for example, chatrooms and text messages) allows instant communication, which is helpful for interacting in real time and when there is some time urgency (for example, while doing homework or studying for an exam). Use of synchronous ICT also promotes active engagement and offers a real sense of interacting with others in the community. The challenge, though, is that synchronous ICT requires that someone is available to communicate at specific times (for example, during virtual office hours) or whenever the need arises (for example, whenever a student is looking for homework help, possibly at 2 A.M.).

Asynchronous ICT, on the other hand, allows people to post a message, through such mechanisms as a discussion board (for example, a forum in which participants post discussions around a particular topic) or a listserv (that is, a group e-mail), whenever it is convenient for them, with the understanding that others will see it and respond whenever it is convenient for them. In asynchronous modalities, people communicate with each other whenever they have the time. Asynchronous communications are then stored so that others can receive the communications and benefit from the information at their convenience. The challenge, however, is that long delays between communications can result in the information becoming less useful and the support less timely. This can result in the VLC becoming less salient and valuable to its members.

Next, we present current communication technologies and how they can be used to create a VLC that supports and extends traditional face-to-face learning communities. As already discussed, although VLCs are considered a "future" or emerging form of learning community, it is quite likely that many, if not most current learning communities incorporate some ICTs already. E-mail, listservs, and websites have become ubiquitous methods of communication within disciplines. In addition, students as well as faculty use a variety of social media (for example, Facebook, Twitter) to connect with one another. For each social technology, we attempt to provide suggestions for the strategic use of the ICTs that are popular with today's college students and can help build a vibrant community. We also use theory and research in social, community, and organizational psychology to help maximize the benefits of VLCs.

Listservs. Listservs are group e-mails in which members send an e-mail to one e-mail address and it is copied and sent to the entire group. We assume that most readers of this chapter as well as most college students have experience with multiple listservs. In a VLC, listservs are perhaps the most basic technology used to send announcements to a class or to the entire community. Although listservs can be helpful mechanisms for sharing information with large numbers of people, they tend not to be sufficiently interactive to be an important community building ICT.

On-Line Bulletin Boards. Bulletin boards are another well-established ICT, although faculty and students are less likely to have experience with these communication technologies. Bulletin boards allow members to have asynchronous discussions about particular topics. What distinguishes them from listservs is that these discussions occur in a particular location (as opposed to arriving in one's e-mail box), and discussions are more easily stored and viewed well after the communication exchange. On-line bulletin boards could be linked to a particular class and used for conducting class discussions or for providing homework help (that is, discussions between the teaching assistant [TA] and the students). In this way, bulletin boards are similar to on-line support already offered by other teaching software such as Blackboard, WebCT, or MOODLE. However, on-line bulletin boards can also support such topics as job and internship postings, text book sales, housing needs and opportunities, or opportunities for involvement in faculty research. Teaching assistants can use bulletin boards to inform students of group study sessions, assignments, campus resources, and other matters. In addition to these practical topics, these on-line bulletin boards can offer opportunities for social interactions such as announcements for psychology-relevant clubs, group social events, intramurals, and other social topics created by and relevant to members of the community.

Although educational software like Blackboard, WebCT, and MOODLE may be common on campuses, VLC developers are advised to explore freeware (such as phpBB[1]) that is used to support other types of virtual communities. This software allows for the creation of multiple discussion boards that can be open to the entire VLC membership as well as private ones for specific subgroups of people (for example, a particular class or a group of students working on a class project). It also allows members to create their own user profiles and to interact privately with other members, both important components of creating community. Indeed, there are several versions of freeware virtual community technology that support nearly all of the ICT we discuss in this section and the cost (free) is appealing to budget-conscious colleges and universities. It does require that someone with information technology skills help set it up and provide occasional maintenance, but such support often can be obtained from your campus technology support services.

Chatrooms. Chatrooms offer the opportunity for synchronous (that is, real-time) interactions for the VLC. For example, faculty, TAs, or academic advisors can hold virtual office hours for students. These office hours can be separate from regular face-to-face office hours, enabling "nontraditional" students to access faculty and TAs in a more flexible way.

Social Networking ICT. These include such readily available technologies as blogs, Facebook, Twitter, and even YouTube videos. Blogs can allow in-depth essays about academic research, the student experience, or general information relevant to the VLC. Blogs tend to be longer than typical bulletin board postings and thus can provide richer details about important topics. In addition, the comments section on the blogs allow for interactions between VLC members about the blog topic. Facebook, which is probably the most common ICT that students use, can also provide an important link for students in a VLC. When students "like" the VLC on Facebook, they will automatically receive status updates on their newsfeeds. Because many students are on Facebook many times a day, this could be an opportunity to publicize bulletin board discussions, blog updates, and even chatroom times. It could even duplicate or even replace the announcements made on the listserv, if enough students "like" the VLC page on Facebook.

Twitter is a growing social networking technology that has some similarities to Facebook. Messages (that is, tweets) are posted on Twitter, and people who follow the VLC Twitter account then receive these messages. Twitter could be used in similar ways to Facebook for providing publicity to blog and discussion board updates. For example, anyone following @UNCCPsychVLC would receive updates and information anytime the person in charge of this account tweets a message. Twitter could also be used, however, for targeted discussions. If the VLC has a dedicated hashtag (for example, #UNCCPsychVLC for the University of North Carolina Charlotte Psychology VLC), then *anyone* could tweet a message using that hashtag and engage in a discussion with others on Twitter. This would include members and nonmembers of the VLC and people who do and do not follow the @UNCCPsychVLC account. Currently, people use hashtags to have time-sensitive discussions, such as tweeting back channel conversations during presentations and events. Truly, the uses of Facebook and Twitter are likely to grow out of the unique interests and needs of the VLC members who are using them. Finally, a YouTube channel is a way for a VLC to post relevant videos (for example, speakers, class presentations, advising sessions); subscribers to the channel are automatically informed of updates and new additions. A YouTube channel dedicated to the VLC could provide access to campus resources, including colloquia by visiting scholars. YouTube could make it increasingly possible for a wide variety of students to benefit from these resources.

Intersections Between Virtual and Other Learning Communities

As discussed previously, VLCs have most frequently occurred in the context of on-line courses or other distance-learning efforts. One example is the innovative hybrid learning community developed for Native American students and offered as a partnership between Grays Harbor College (GHC) and the Evergreen State College (TESC) in Washington state (Hardiman, Smith, Washington, and Brewster, 2007). The hybrid VLC combines a degree program delivered on-line with many face-to-face elements delivered on-site at participating Indian reservations. Although this hybrid VLC is not discipline centered, it frequently serves to create connections among students, faculty, and curricula within the academic majors of its members, including psychology. Clearly, the innovative use of information and computer technologies drives the success of such interinstitutional hybrid learning communities.

Indeed, VLCs can be used to augment and enhance the reach and impact of any type of learning community previously discussed in this volume (that is, curriculum based, classroom based, residential based, or student based). First, for classroom-based LCs, VLCs can provide a comprehensive system to enhance the interaction and communication among students, between students and teaching assistants, and between students and faculty. In this type of VLC, one might find on-line office hours, discussions of class topics that could occur outside of class and perhaps even spontaneous discussions of class assignments among students or between students and the professor. This type of VLC may be the easiest for people new to virtual communities to comprehend and implement because it is merely an augmentation of what currently occurs. It is also time limited because it occurs around a particular class.

A VLC connected to a student-based learning community might take on a different form. Because these types of VLC are connected to particular student groups (for example, Psi Chi, a psychology club, or peer advisors) and exist alongside or as part of that group, they are similar to the classroom-based VLCs discussed earlier. However, they are not bounded by any particular time period and continue to exist with the student group as long as they are useful. Similar to the classroom-based VLCs, the technologies associated with these VLCs could facilitate discussion as well as serve as a space for posting of announcements. Although faculty may serve as advisors to the student group and would interact with students in that role, these VLCs would primarily be for students to interact with one another.

A third type of VLC could be linked to curriculum-based LCs. Here we envision a VLC that exists across courses and over time, with the potential for extending a first-year learning community (LC) all the way through graduation for its members. For example, during the first year of a curriculum-centered LC, a VLC is established that links faculty, staff, and students across the courses in the first-year curriculum. These links would provide a secondary support for both the academic and social functions of the LC, providing a useful vehicle for integrative assignments, information sharing, and virtual connections throughout the first year.

One of the goals of the first-year experience is to prepare students for the next three years as they move into their specialized area of interest and pursue experiences (for example, internships, research opportunities, study abroad, and so on) appropriate to upper-class students. During the first year, the VLC might be used to help students develop these specialized interests (for example, links to university career centers, on-line interest inventories, links to faculty within subdisciplinary areas) and link them to other students with similar academic and career interests within the major. Then, during the next three years, students would transition into one of several VLCs that are designed to extend the LC experience based on their specialized interests. For example, we envision separate VLCs for second-, third-, and fourth-year students that group students around subdisciplinary interests such as industrial–organizational (I–O) psychology, clinical psychology, community psychology, and so on. Each VLC would serve the role of helping students and faculty with those interests connect with one another and interact around topics specific to those content areas. This same model could be used in departments without a first-year LC; for example, undergraduates who enroll in a series of courses in a neuropsychology concentration might be invited to participate in the neuropsychology VLC, which could provide a forum to discuss relevant research and media topics while also allowing students to interact outside of class. Internships and job opportunities as well as advising could be provided in this VLC, too. Although we are not aware of any departments using this particular approach to VLCs, the possibilities seem limitless.

Finally, VLCs could complement residential LCs to help build cohesiveness among a cohort of new students or to help integrate them into a multiyear group of residents. The VLC could include broader university resources, helping ensure that the students are aware of them and increasing the likelihood that students from the LC would participate in those activities together. The VLC could be limited to the time students are in the residential LC or could extend in time to help students maintain their links to other students and staff throughout their tenure at the university. Multiple options exist for such a VLC that could include helping a cohort of students progress through their degrees together, developing relationships, and creating a strong feeling of community within their cohort. Of course, an ambitious department could set up a comprehensive VLC that incorporates any or all of the examples presented here to meet their specific needs. Indeed, one of the most exciting aspects of ICT is that often imagination and a needs assessment can come together to create a new on-line interactive group that successfully fills an important void.

In spite of the many instances where technology is used to supplement and extend other types of discipline-centered learning communities, we could not find any examples of a stand-alone VLC in psychology to feature in this chapter. Thus, we would like to articulate a vision of what such a VLC might look like and reflect on several issues for psychology departments interested in developing one. We envision a psychology VLC that could engage all students throughout their entire time in the major, with subcomponents that are specific to particular courses, clubs, cohorts, or other subgroups. Ideally, the VLC would be as real and central to the learning experience of the students as the psychology building in which they take their classes. Although this would certainly take considerable effort to start, perhaps due more to the need to change habits of faculty and staff, we believe that this could become a normal and essential part of their university experience once the VLC is operational and moves to maintenance mode.

To create such a VLC, we would begin with a comprehensive site like the phpBB bulletin board we described earlier. There would be secure sections open only to particular subsets of students (for example, freshmen), which would help socialize students into college life as a psychology major. Student clubs and groups could also have sections, which would be open to all members and would send out automated e-mail announcements to all students about upcoming events. Individual classes could also have secure sections in which students interact with each other and TAs and professors hold office hours. Other sections could be available based on the needs and the imagination of the department including buying and selling books, advice on internships, research opportunities, and jobs, advising information, and even social opportunities like clubs or cultural or sports activities. Essentially, we are suggesting that such a VLC could incorporate many of the other types of LCs that are common in psychology departments, but it would be centralized into one supporting technology. These could then serve as supportive infrastructure for other, more traditional, types of LCs.

Benefits of VLCs

There are many benefits of VLCs. Clearly, they can easily facilitate connections among students, faculty, advisors, and other stakeholders within an academic discipline in a cost-effective manner. One well-documented benefit of increased connections is the sense of community (McMillan and Chavis, 1986) experienced by participants, particularly the students. A sense of community refers to the feelings of belonging, identity, and attachment that develop among the students vis-à-vis one another, their department, their university, and their major. Developing a sense of community is a major goal of both face-to-face learning communities (Daniel, Schwier, and Ross, 2007) and VLCs (Nolan and Weiss, 2002), as well as virtual communities focused on a variety of topics outside of a learning environment (for example, Blanchard, 2004; Lev-On, 2010; Rheingold, 1993). Indeed, over the past decade, a sense of virtual community (SOVC) construct has attracted growing attention (Blanchard, 2008; Blanchard and Markus, 2004; Koh and Kim, 2003). SOVC is based on the well-established construct of sense of community in face-to-face communities, which was developed and examined in community psychology (McMillan and Chavis, 1986). SOVC is particularly important for examining VLCs because of its relation to important outcomes for members, including retention, problem solving, reduced stress, and increased trust (Blanchard and others, 2011; McMillan and Chavis, 1986; Welbourne, Blanchard, and Boughton, 2009).

A second major benefit of VLCs is enabling students to participate in departmental activities from a distance or at times that are not convenient for face-to-face interactions. As opposed to residential learning communities, which require that students live on campus, VLCs can help build connections between the student and the department and among students at times and locations that are possible for the students. Particularly important for the growing numbers of nontraditional students (for example, older students, students with families, transfers from community colleges), VLCs allow students to "attend" departmental colloquia via YouTube, or "attend" virtual office hours while being home with children or during breaks from their jobs in distant communities. Because increasing numbers of students are also likely to be taking on-line or hybrid (partially on-line) courses, a VLC can facilitate their communication with their peers, to provide mutual aid through on-line study groups or chat rooms.

A third major benefit of VLCs is derived from the substantial evidence that on-line communication allows for greater participation and voice for traditionally underrepresented members such as women, minorities, or lesbian, gay, bisexual, and transsexual individuals (Culnan and Markus, 1987; Kiesler, Seigel, and McGuire, 1984; Wellman and Guilia, 1999). By making it more possible for minority and underrepresented students to have a voice and participate more fully in departmental and university life, and therefore to feel a greater sense of community within the department, VLCs can likely help universities increase the diversity of their student bodies and increase the likelihood that these groups will be successful and graduate.

How to Build Successful VLCs

This leads to the next important step in understanding VLCs—how to build them successfully. A very common, yet incorrect, assumption about the creation of on-line groups is: If we build it, they will come. Many interactive group technologies fail when developers assume that the technology is inherently of value and will be used because it can potentially serve some useful purpose. Clearly, this assumption is incorrect and can easily lead to wasted time and effort for anyone developing a VLC.

Fortunately, there is a broad literature within community psychology and information science which provides advice on creating successful new groups. The creation of a successful VLC requires (a) identification of student needs, (b) engagement of students (and other participants) in the development of the VLC to address those needs, and (c) evaluation of how well the specific components of the VLC help students connect with other students and faculty, receive needed support, develop appropriate behaviors and skills, and successfully complete their programs of study.

Each step is critical in developing and sustaining a successful VLC. For example, if students do not see a need for or desire the VLC, then they will be unlikely to participate. Engaging the intended participants (students, faculty, and any others) in the planning of the VLC is critical to ensure that it will meet their needs and will be convenient and fit well into the existing culture of the university and department. Although students are generally the primary beneficiaries and participants in VLCs, faculty are also important actors in the process. As such, the community must be designed to fit the needs and interests of both students and faculty, within the contextual limitations and advantages of the university setting. Planning for a new VLC should make sure to identify mechanisms that build both interaction and identity.

Interaction. Interaction among members is an essential feature of virtual communities (Rheingold, 1993) and for the development of an SOVC (Blanchard, 2004, 2008; Koh and Kim, 2003; Lev-On, 2010). The interactions among members can focus on informational and/or socioemotional exchange, both of which can be important benefits of a VLC. For example, a VLC is likely to be a good source of information related to coursework, discipline-specific topics, or job opportunities. Exchange of information can then lead to the exchange of socioemotional support (Blanchard, Askay, and Callas, 2010; Blanchard and Markus, 2004). Although some faculty may not see the value of "social" uses of ICT, these uses are often viewed as highly important by students and can facilitate accomplishment of academic goals. For example, nonacademic factors such as perceived institutional commitment, social support, and involvement have been found to be highly influential in student retention, particularly for women and minority students (Lotkowski, Robbins, and Noeth, 2004). VLCs might be particularly useful because they can readily contribute to both academic and non-academic factors that increase student success.

A specific benefit of VLCs compared to other LCs is that the support exchanged by a few people within the community is viewed by and perhaps felt by a much larger number of people (Wellman and Guilia, 1999). This means that everyone can benefit from questions and answers about a particular topic, even if only a few people actually post information about it. This small act of helping becomes a larger one as everyone in the community reads it. It also promotes a perception of helpfulness that can benefit the entire VLC.

Identity. The creation of an identity is also critical in the development of VLCs. This includes members learning the identity of others and developing their own identity. As members learn about one another and develop their own identities, a group identity among the members also develops which is a key to the success of virtual communities (Postmes, Spears, Lee, and Novak, 2005). One way to develop a personal identity is through interaction. When members post messages in the group, others begin to recognize their voice (Postmes and others, 2005) and develop an impression of them (Walther and Burgoon, 1992; Walther, Slovacek, and Tidwell, 2001). In addition, the use of identification technologies (that is, avatars, pictures, signature files, participation information) can also foster the development of personal identities (Walther and others, 2001). Therefore, it is important for virtual communities to include technological features that provide information about the participants (for example, how long they have been a member, how many times they have posted, their role in the group such as moderator or teaching assistant) as well as technology that can be modified by the user to provide information (for example, a signature file for identifying information, external web links or pithy statements, avatars and pictures, and so on).

It is important to note that developing opportunities for interaction is essential both for the exchange of support and creating and learning identities. Nonetheless, the creation of "opportunities" for interaction, even with topics of high interest to the students, does not preclude the VLC falling into the "If we build it, they will come" trap. It is important for VLC developers, at least at the beginning of the VLC life, to seed discussions and conversations. For example, a prominent student or professor with good on-line communication skills can help lead discussions and answer questions. In addition, departments, advisors, and faculty can post important information on the VLC, with frequent updates, to encourage students to visit the VLC and perhaps even "hang out" a bit. Making the VLC the way to find out about important information can encourage student visits. A key here is what is meant by "frequent." Posting information once a semester would be a death knell to an on-line site. Even once a week may not be frequent enough for students used to checking their Facebook statuses many times a day. Although this investment will be costly early on in the life of the VLC, the payback will be a student-run, self-sustaining VLC in the future.

A Look Ahead

The lack of examples of VLCs in psychology found in the literature, given that over a decade has passed since Lenning and Ebbers (1999) introduced the concept of a VLC, is certainly not due to limits in technology, financial constraints, or student unwillingness to use ICTs. We suspect that the limited use of VLCs in psychology is a function of the limited ability or willingness of psychology faculty to embrace newer technologies that foster student–faculty and student–student interactions. While adoption of newer technologies can require considerable investments in time, the benefits can be significant, allowing faculty to hold office hours from anywhere, addressing questions that one student might raise at any time with the entire class, fostering small group interactions that strengthen learning, engaging more students in research, better preparing students for graduate school ... the list could go on. Of course, these are potential benefits, and we should take care to evaluate their impacts on faculty and students. But certainly many faculty can remember a time when e-mail was a new technology, and although it can be the bane of our existence in some ways, we might also wonder how we could do our jobs without it. Given the increasing dependence of our students on technology, its growing availability and accessibility, shrinking budgets in higher education and the quest to find more economical but effective ways to enhance learning outcomes, it seems likely that VLCs will proliferate academic departments in the near future.

Certainly the technologies continue to change, and adoption of any given technology entails the risk that it will soon be obsolete. However, most of the resources mentioned here have been in place for several years and have continued to be useful. In the next decade, there will inevitably be changes in both the technologies and their use. Inevitably, though, ICTs will continue to become more widely used, mainstream communication options. As they become increasingly integrated into the lives of our students and faculty, psychology departments would wisely take advantage of them to develop thriving VLCs for their students.

References

Blanchard, A. L. "Blogs as Virtual Communities: Identifying Sense of Community in the Julie/Julia Project." In L. Gurak, and others (eds.), *Into the Blogosphere: Rhetoric, Community and Culture.* 2004. Retrieved August 10, 2012, from http://blog.lib.umn.edu/blogosphere/blogs_as_virtual.html.

Blanchard, A. L. "Testing a Model of Sense of Virtual Community." *Computers in Human Behavior,* 2008, 24, 2107–2123.

Blanchard, A. L., Askay, D., and Callas. "Sense of Community in Professional Virtual Communities." In S. D. Long (ed.), *Communication, Relationships, and Practices in Virtual Work.* Hershey, Pa.: IGI Global, 2010.

Blanchard, A. L., and Markus, M. L. . "The Experienced 'Sense' of a Virtual Community: Characteristics and Processes." *The DATA BASE for Advances in Information Systems,* 2004, *35*(1), 65–79.

Blanchard, A. L., Welbourne, J. A., and Boughton, M. D. "A Model of Trust: The Mediating Role of Norms and Sense of Virtual Community." *Information, Communication and Technology,* 2011, *14*(1), 76–106.

Culnan, M. J., and Markus, M. L. "Information Technologies: Electronic Media and Interorganizational Communication." In F. M. Jablin, L. L. Putnam, K. H. Roberts, and L. W. Porter (eds.), *Handbook of Organizational Communication: An Interdisciplinary Perspective* (pp. 420–443). Newbury Park, Calif.: Sage, 1987.

Daniel, B. K., Schwier, R. A., and Ross, H. M. "Synthesis of the Process of Learning through Discourse in a Formal Virtual Learning Community." *Journal of Interactive Learning Research,* 2007, *18*(4), 461–477.

Hardiman, J., Smith, B. L., Washington, K., and Brewster, E. "Connecting with Local Communities: The Evergreen State College." In B. L. Smith and L. B. Williams (eds.), *Learning Communities and Student Affairs: Partnering for Powerful Learning* (pp. 87–102). Olympia, Wash.: Washington Center for Improving the Quality of Undergraduate Education, The Evergreen State College, 2007.

Kiesler, S., Seigel, J., and McGuire, T. "Social Psychological Aspects of Computer-Mediated Communication." *American Psychologist,* 1984, *39*(10), 1123–1134.

Koh, J., and Kim, Y.-G. "Sense of Virtual Community: A Conceptual Framework and Empirical Validation." *International Journal of Electronic Commerce,* 2003, *8*(2), 75.

Lenning, O. T., and Ebbers, L. H. *The Powerful Potential of Learning Communities: Improving Education for the Future.* ASHE-ERIC Higher Education Report, Vol. 26, No. 6. Washington, D.C.: George Washington University, 1999.

Lev-On, A. "Engaging the Disengaged: Collective Action, Media Uses, and Sense of (Virtual) Community by Evacuees from Gush Katif." *American Behavioral Scientist,* 2010, *53*(8), 1208–1227. doi: 10.1177/0002764209356251

Lotkowski, V. A., Robbins, S. B., and Noeth, R. J. *The Role of Academic and Non-Academic Factors in Improving College Retention.* ACT Policy Report. Iowa City, Iowa: ACT, Inc., 2004.

McMillan, D. W., and Chavis, D. M. "Sense of Community: A Definition and Theory." *Journal of Community Psychology,* 1986, *14*(1), 6–23.

Nolan, D. J., and Weiss, J. "Learning in Cyberspace: An Educational View of Virtual Community." In K. A. Renninger and W. Shumar (eds.), *Building Virtual Communities: Learning and Change in Cyberspace* (pp. 293–320). New York: Cambridge University Press, 2002.

Postmes, T., Spears, R., Lee, A. T., and Novak, R., J. "Individuality and Social Influence in Groups: Inductive and Deductive Routes to Group Identity." *Journal of Personality and Social Psychology,* 2005, *89*(5), 747–763.

Rheingold, H. *The Virtual Community: Homesteading on the Electronic Frontier.* Reading, Mass.: Addison-Wesley, 1993.

Walther, J. B., and Burgoon, J. K. "Relational Communication in Computer-Mediated Interaction." *Human Communication Research,* 1992, *19*(1), 50–88.

Walther, J. B., Slovacek, C. L., and Tidwell, L. C. "Is a Picture Worth a Thousand Words?: Photographic Images in Long-Term and Short-Term Computer-Mediated Communication." *Communication Research,* 2001, *28*(1), 105–134.

Welbourne, J. A., Blanchard, A. L., and Boughton, M. D. *Supportive Communication, Sense of Virtual Community and Health Outcomes in Online Infertility Groups.* Paper presented at the Communities and Technology 2007: Proceedings of the Fourth

Communities and Technologies Conference, Pennsylvania State University, University Park, 2009.

Wellman, B., and Guilia, M. "Net Surfers Don't Ride Alone: Virtual Communities as Communities." In B. Wellman (ed.), *Networks in the Global Village: Life in Contemporary Communities* (pp. 331–366). Boulder, Colo.: Westview, 1999.

Note

1. phpBB is easily found with a Google search. We have no affiliation with this group and indeed there are others out there. Nonetheless, we have found this particular virtual community hosting software easy to use and modify for our purposes.

ANITA L. BLANCHARD *is associate professor of psychology and organizational science at the University of North Carolina at Charlotte.*

JAMES R. COOK *is professor of psychology and community psychologist at the University of North Carolina at Charlotte.*

NEW DIRECTIONS FOR TEACHING AND LEARNING • DOI: 10.1002/tl

8

In 1990, the current authors with Faith Gabelnick authored their first book about learning community initiatives, which has gone on to become one of the most widely cited volumes in the New Directions for Teaching and Learning series. In this chapter, they reflect on the developments and evolution of learning communities since that time, including their reflections on each chapter from the present volume.

The Evolution of Learning Communities: A Retrospective

Roberta S. Matthews, Barbara Leigh Smith, Jean MacGregor

This volume, so ably assembled by Kim Buch and Kenneth Barron, focuses on learning communities at the beginning and at the culmination of work in the major of psychology and reflects a commitment to good practice both within and outside the classroom. Its comprehensive approach attests to the power of learning communities within the discipline and is a fine example of their evolution. As part of this effort, we welcome the opportunity to look at the development of learning communities over the years, the growth and diversification of these approaches, and the good practices that have emerged. At the same time, our reflections stimulated a number of questions whose consideration would, we believe, help strengthen the learning communities movement.

Learning Communities as a Maturing Movement

When we wrote our first book about curricular learning communities (Gabelnick and others, 1990), these programs were beginning to spread, but we had no idea how pervasive they would become over the next twenty years. Multiple varieties of learning community programs are now commonplace in all types of colleges and universities across the United States. Indeed, learning communities may be described as a maturing movement. Many educational innovations, even promising ones, never fully scale up to reach their full potential on a single campus or become a widespread feature of many campuses; the good news is that learning communities have

New Directions for Teaching and Learning, no. 132, Winter 2012 © Wiley Periodicals, Inc.
Published online in Wiley Online Library (wileyonlinelibrary.com) • DOI: 10.1002/tl.20039

done both. Learning community approaches continue to evolve and expand in their scope and potential for addressing significant educational challenges.

Early learning community initiatives often began as labor-intensive efforts led by small groups of heroically dedicated faculty and staff, frequently in opposition to established patterns and institutional assumptions and almost always against the grain. Of necessity, program leaders focused their energies on getting their learning community programs established and accepted on their campuses. Although many of these small pockets of excellence failed to grow, others succeeded by evolving into broadly based and intentionally focused reform efforts. As learning community programs developed and won the support of institutional leaders, colleges and universities focused on institutionalizing their programs and strengthening program quality and program assessment. Furthermore, many campuses began to make intentional efforts to address problem areas in the curriculum, to better meet student needs, and to increase the quality of student engagement and learning.

At the same time, at higher education conferences of all kinds, learning community leaders began to create a national conversation about different learning community approaches and best practices. By the late 1990s and early 2000s, a substantial learning community literature began to emerge (Hurd and Stein, 2004; Shapiro and Levine, 1999). Taken together, these developments contributed to more intentional practices related to learning community curriculum, pedagogy, implementation, and assessment.

Today, learning communities reach substantial numbers of students. Strong learning community initiatives flourish in developmental education, first-year experience programs and general education, study in the major, master's-degree programs, on-line learning, honors courses, and residence hall experiences. At hundreds of institutions, learning communities are now offered on predictable planning cycles, enjoy identifiable leadership and teaching teams, and benefit from ongoing program assessment—all indicators that these programs have moved from innovation to established reform (Geri and others, 1999; Lardner and Malnarich, 2008b).

Patterns of Evolution, Practice, and Support

In the early decades of curricular learning community development—the 1970s through the 1990s—these programs understandably focused on the freshman year and general education. Learning community pioneers created these programs to increase student retention and also to bring coherence to general education coursework.

Our own work with learning communities concentrated on the first two years of college as well. Based on our instincts and experiences, as well as the work of Patricia Cross (1971), Arthur Chickering and Zelda Gamson

NEW DIRECTIONS FOR TEACHING AND LEARNING • DOI: 10.1002/tl

(1987), Vince Tinto (1987), and Lee Upcraft and John Gardner and the First-Year Experience (1989), we understood how crucial were the first two years of college and how students' experience during this time either committed them to or ushered them out the ("revolving") door of higher education—vividly reflected in seemingly intractable dropout rates. In his landmark book, *Leaving College: Rethinking the Causes and Cures of Student Attrition*, first published in 1987, Vincent Tinto pointed out that the window of opportunity to retain first-year students was basically the first six weeks of the first semester. His work drew national attention to the critical nature of a student's introduction to college, especially those who were the most fragile and least likely to succeed.

For us, two obstacles to students' academic success stood out: the bone-crushing boredom of developmental courses detached from meaningful college-level content, at worst a series of "skills and drills" exercises separated from their essential context; and the reduction of general education to a series of check-off requirements that too many students trudged through, rarely noting anything of inherent interest or practical use in the smorgasbord of courses that their particular institution of higher education made them take, for reasons that often remained unclear. In different ways, each introductory higher education experience offered problems and obstacles that could be resolved by thoughtfully constructed learning communities. For practical reasons, we focused on learning communities as vehicles for developing and enriching inter- and multidisciplinary experiences for students that would help convince them they were "college material" and also that higher education was an adventure they wished to undertake and continue.

And so we advocated the creation of thematic learning communities among skills courses, and also, to the horror of some, learning communities that linked skills and content courses so students would see the importance of skills related to their own areas of interest. Linking general education courses yielded rich and resonant themes and areas of connection. In both cases, the goal was to develop essential skills in the context of intellectual stimulation and growth and in a community of one's peers and teachers.

Two national higher education associations played a significant role in promoting the learning communities approach. During the decades of the 1980s and '90s, the American Association of Higher Education (AAHE) served as an intellectual incubator as well as an early site for learning communities' dissemination. For many years, the AAHE identified, defined, and created the "big ideas" in higher education; their national conferences were a venue for all kinds of intellectual stimulation and networking. We were active contributors to AAHE, and our thinking was enriched and deepened by our encounters and experiences within that organization. Similarly, the Association of American Colleges and Universities (AAC&U) has supported and enriched national conversations about liberal education and, in that context, has also heavily influenced the learning community move-ment. The AAC&U is now into its sixth year of a ten-year Liberal Educa-tion and America's Promise (LEAP) project (2007). The LEAP project created and developed "Essential Learning Outcomes" that encompass and reflect consultation within academe and the business community—a com-prehensive statement of common and general education goals that empha-size enduring skills and abilities. A related AAC&U project, VALUE, or Valid Assessment of Learning in Undergraduate Education, has developed assessment rubrics for fifteen generic intellectual and practical, personal and social responsibility, and integrative and applied learning skills.

At the same time, several public and private foundations were crucial to supporting early learning community development, assessment, and dis-semination. The Comprehensive Program of the Fund for the Improvement of Post-Secondary Education (FIPSE) funded many of the first learning community experiments in the eastern United States in the 1970s and the Washington Center for Improving the Quality of Undergraduate Educa-tion's first national dissemination project in the late 1990s. The National Science Foundation's Division of Undergraduate Education supported learning community initiatives in science, engineering, and mathematics. The federally funded National Center for Postsecondary Teaching, Learn-ing, and Assessment at Pennsylvania State University supported the first comprehensive multi-institutional research projects on learning commu-nity programs (Tinto and others, 1994).

The Pew Charitable Trusts supported a large-scale learning community initiative at Temple University, and later, the Washington Center's National Learning Communities Dissemination Project. Federal Title III and Title V grants have consistently supported learning community development tar-geted at low-income or first-generation students.

New Partnerships and Shared Goals

First-Year Seminars, advocated by John Gardner and his colleagues and ubiquitous today in higher education, were introduced in the 1970s and scaled up with the support of the First-Year Experience Conferences during the '80s and '90s. During this time first-year seminars were linked with first-year curricular learning communities focusing on the skills or compo-sition and general education courses typical of first-year programs. Such linkages allowed students to use the time management, study skills, and other strategies for success in various courses in the context of real aca-demic requirements (Henscheid, 2004).

As curricular learning communities began to proliferate, partnerships emerged between academic and student affairs divisions to strengthen both the *learning* and the *community* aspects of learning community programs (Smith, Williams, and others, 2007). Residential learning communities appeared in multiple forms, from thematic residence halls to team-taught academic programs. Saint Lawrence University was one of the first to develop an extensive residential learning community model for its entire freshman class, which brought faculty members and student affairs professionals together as teaching teams. Among many others, universities such as Iowa State, University of Missouri, University of Massachusetts-Amherst, and University of Maryland built substantial living-learning community initiatives.

Along with the new alliances among curricular learning communities, freshman-year programming, academic advising, and residence life, we have seen creative partnerships with other important campus initiatives. Numerous learning community programs are now well integrated with service learning and civic-engagement initiatives (MacGregor, 2003). Librarians have joined learning community teaching teams (Pedersen, 2003). Interdisciplinary field–semesters, such as Saint Lawrence's Adirondack Semester and Whitman's Semester in the West, and, more recently, numerous study-abroad learning community programs offer extraordinary opportunities for integrated learning in rich experiential contexts. Love's opening chapter in this volume aptly describes learning communities as a key strategy for "leveraging a number of components (and ideas) crucial to student learning and development." As she points out, much of the success of the movement is due to its grounding in and advocacy of proven high-impact core practices of student learning.

Comprehensive and residential learning communities in psychology reaching out to new students are a logical extension of these trends in higher education, a practical and proactive response of a discipline. These first-year learning communities, coordinated across all areas, extend a welcome to new students with a stated interest in psychology and provide them with a rich and supportive introduction to the discipline, as described in the chapters by Zrull, Rocheleau, Smith, and Bergman and by Grills, Fingerhut, Thadani, and Machón.

At the other end of the spectrum, the ongoing and thoughtful work of the faculty partners Nolan and Jenkins in their senior seminar in psychology underscores that, for engaged faculty, curriculum is always a work in progress. The challenges addressed in this culminating seminar look beyond the walls of academe to the work experiences of graduates and underscore both the difficulty and necessity of addressing the often fundamental gap between higher education and the world of work. That the discipline must prepare its graduates for a wide spectrum of related work experiences as well as for graduate school, and that the former is a challenge in ways that the latter is not, is an important lesson for all disciplines.

The National Collegiate Honors Council (NCHC), one of whose founders was our colleague Faith Gabelnick, is a pioneering national organization for honors programs and one of the first national conferences to give students an opportunity to present their research alongside other students and professors. Over the years, honors programs and clubs—both disciplinary and institutional—have proliferated and taken seriously their roles of enriching the higher education experiences of very capable students, while at the same time providing honors students with opportunities to contribute to their communities, whether it be in their departments, particular institutions, or local schools and communities. The growth of honors programs and the development of models to accommodate institutional need are reflected in this volume as well, in the chapter written by Hall.

All these partnerships have reconceived and expanded the notions of who plays important teaching roles at a college or university and where learning can occur. No doubt in recognition of the growing belief that academic and student affairs needed to better coordinate their activities to serve the students they shared, it is telling to us that over the years, the phrase "extracurricular" has evolved to "cocurricular."

Assessment

In this maturing movement, we see serious assessment work, and, most important, using this work to inform practice. High-quality assessment is evident at both the planning stages for many learning community programs and used for the purposes of evaluating and improving programs. The wealth of data sources on best practices and extensive collaborative work on standards takes many forms. Colleges and universities can now choose from an array of nationally administered and normed assessment instruments as well as homegrown instruments that provide good information about the institutions and their students.

Learning communities have now been studied from many different perspectives, and the promising results of these programs helped to catapult the learning community strategy into national attention. The multi-institutional research of Vincent Tinto and his colleagues in the early 1990s was especially important in this regard (Tinto and others, 1994) as was subsequent research completed by Cathy Engstrom and her associates (2007 and 2008). In 2003, as part of the Washington Center's National Learning Communities Project, a research team led by Kathe Taylor synthesized the findings of 32 dissertations and research studies and 119 learning community program assessment reports in a monograph that demonstrated the potential of learning communities for student engagement and success and also made recommendations for strengthening learning community assessment and assessment reports. George Kuh's more recent monograph, *High-Impact Educational Practices: What They Are, Who Has Access to Them, and Why They Matter* (2008), written under the aegis of the AAC&U LEAP project, documents practices such as first-year seminars, learning communities, undergraduate research, and service learning that colleges commonly and successfully use to enrich liberal education and improve the academic outcomes of their students. The inclusion of learning communities in Kuh's monograph and in national surveys such as the National Survey of Student Engagement (NSSE) and the Community College Survey of Student Engagement (CCSSE) attest to their broad reach and documented impact. More recently, the MDRC has initiated a series of multi-institutional studies on learning community programs that explicitly serve underprepared students (Visher and others, 2010).

The chapters in this volume reflect an extraordinarily significant transformation in higher education, that of thoughtful and focused assessment as the means to demonstrate success and identify areas needing improvement. This is something we would not have seen fifteen years ago. Although dedicated to exploring learning communities within a discipline, this volume nevertheless reflects and cites a wide range of research and assessment on learning communities. For those of us who began with homegrown student questionnaires, the proliferation of doctoral dissertations, formal studies, national assessment tools specifically for learning communities, and their positioning within larger areas of concern to higher education are impressive developments.

Inter-institutional Partnerships and Networks

An additional, major element of the maturation of the learning community movement is the emergence of regional and national inter-institutional efforts to build a national community of practice that has, in turn, further stimulated and strengthened programmatic practices. There are active listservs for practitioners in learning communities and living-learning programs. The Washington Center hosts a rich website that provides extensive learning community resources, including an on-line directory of learning community programs and an emerging Learning Communities Research and Practice e-Journal. Regional learning communities networks in the Mid-Atlantic States, Illinois, Washington, and California hold periodic conferences and curriculum planning retreats. The Washington Center hosts an annual Summer Institute on Learning Communities for campus teams. The annual National Learning Communities Conference, begun by Delta College in 1996 and now in its seventeenth year, is sponsored by a consortium of six diverse colleges and universities; each year, this conference draws hundreds of faculty members, student affairs professionals, assessment staff, and administrative leaders to share successful approaches and address challenges in learning communities implementation.

Assessment, association, and their articulation in articles and presentations have worked synergistically to build learning communities as a maturing movement: a robust literature and a variety of venues serve as occasions for practitioners to share ideas, work through challenges, and stimulate new work.

NEW DIRECTIONS FOR TEACHING AND LEARNING • DOI: 10.1002/tl

Pedagogy with Purpose

The same attention to detail necessary to effect large-scale change is seen as well in the evolution of learning community classrooms. For us, how content was being delivered was almost as important as what was being delivered. As the learning community movement grew, so, too, did attention to pedagogies of active and collaborative learning in order to foster community and to explore and assert connections among different disciplines and ways of knowing. The exploration of rich content and complex ideas has always required more than a passive approach to learning. We are pleased that active pedagogies are detailed in this volume by Saville, Lawrence, and Jakobsen as an essential part of the entire learning community experience.

Our own writings on active learning support the link between the learning community structure and the kind of learning that was occurring within that structure (Smith, MacGregor, Matthews, and Gabelnick, 2004; Smith and MacGregor, 1992; MacGregor, 1990; Matthews, 1995; Matthews, Cooper, Davidson, and Hawkes, 1995). Our conviction of the strong connection between them cannot be overestimated. Because advances in cognitive science have been applied to how people learn (Bransford and others, 1999), the value of active pedagogies is now widely acknowledged; those who ignore these findings exist in increasing intellectual and pedagogical isolation. Moreover, recent work in integrative learning in higher education spearheaded by Washington Center codirectors Emily Lardner and Gillies Malnarich in association with Veronica Boix-Mansilla, a principal investigator at Harvard's Project Zero, has highlighted the necessity of enabling students to explore and articulate the connections as well as differences among and within disciplines and ways of knowing (Boix-Mansilla, 2005; Dunlap and Sult, 2009; Lardner and Malnarich, 2008a). As a community of practice, we need to continue to strengthen these pedagogies of active engagement, collaborative learning, and integrative learning in learning community programs.

Substantial emphasis on faculty and institutional development has been important in building lasting learning community initiatives. By-products of such development include more intentional approaches to teaching, more attuned to changing realities as reflected in various contexts throughout the chapters in the book. Looking back we see the footprints of learning community leaders who "stayed the course" over many years to establish and nurture learning communities on their campuses—faculty, administrators, and professional staff who saw promise in this idea and made it a reality in their institutions at the same time as they incorporated new ideas in teaching and learning with new developments in their disciplines.

Next Steps, Future Directions, and Prospects

Although general education continues to be the largest arena for learning communities, we now see learning communities moving into other curricular venues. Thanks to the path-breaking work of Vincent Tinto, Cathy Engstrom, Emily Lardner, and Gillies Malnarich, learning communities are increasingly being positioned to address problem areas in the curriculum plagued by consistent patterns of student withdrawal and failure. Targeted are "high-risk courses," "critical filter courses," or "graveyard courses," characterized by some as the "killing fields of higher education," where large numbers of students withdraw or fail because they are poorly prepared for the expectations and pace of these courses and are often unfamiliar with a particular disciplinary discourse and culture. Many emerging learning community initiatives link a specially developed and focused skills course to a "high risk" course in a discipline, and the teaching team often includes academic advisors and study-skills or reading specialists (Malnarich and others, 2003).

Recently, focused learning communities in the major have emerged. This volume represents the first book (we hope of many) detailing the development of learning communities in one popular academic major—psychology—and attests to the creativity of practitioners and the variety of venues available within a discipline to implement comprehensive learning communities, supportive pedagogies, and related cocurricular venues and activities.

Another emerging trend is the development of virtual learning communities using on-line learning, as explored in this volume by Blanchard and Cook. On some campuses, as many as one-third of all students take on-line courses. Learning communities are being designed to take advantage of this new mode of designing and delivering curriculum. One trend in e-learning designs is hybrid courses that combine on-line learning with face-to-face elements. Grays Harbor College in Washington has devised an entire associate of arts degree as a virtual learning community for Native students at six rural reservation sites (Hardiman and others, 2007). A hybrid model, this program includes face-to-face elements with local study leaders, a monthly face-to-face class, and a culturally relevant curriculum. Skagit Valley College, where learning communities are required for transfer degrees, also offers a number of virtual learning communities.

Institutions are now moving to codify best practices to strengthen learning community quality. The Evergreen State College and New Century College at George Mason University have institutionalized and codified effective practices through mission statements, clearly articulated standards of good practice, and ongoing faculty development programs. These best practices often take the form of broadly adopting and carefully promoting promising pedagogies such as active learning, collaborative learning, and reflection on learning with such strategies as classroom assessment techniques, reflective tutorials, and e-portfolios. Best practices guidelines are now also available for the design and delivery of on-line courses.

As we look to the future of learning communities in higher education, we are mindful that although learning community initiatives have grown, proliferated, and become more sophisticated over time, no reform endeavor is ever static. At every institution, leadership teams must think about how to keep their learning community programs effective and fresh for everyone involved. Here are some questions that we hope both seasoned and emerging leaders will engage:

- What do students need to learn in college to live and work as contributing citizens in the twenty-first century? How can learning communities address these challenges?
- Could we create faculty interest groups to identify and address issues in different majors? Is there a readiness to embrace new approaches? Are students in majors sufficiently proficient in terms of college-level skills in writing, quantitative reasoning, oral communication, and working in teams? How can learning communities in the major contribute to the development of such skills?
- How can learning communities support our general education programs and help them meet essential student learning outcomes?
- Are there other convergent opportunities to build learning communities around potentially related enterprises such as service learning, diversity, and global education?
- What assessment practices will push us to the next horizon and help us learn from our experiences?
- How do we sustain programs over the long haul through budget cycles and in the face of leadership and faculty turnover? Is transition planning firmly in place? Are the right people on board? How consistent are results? Do rewards support good work?

Based on our experience working with both faculty and administrators in colleges and universities across the country, the act of creating and sustaining learning communities is in itself a community-building experience for an institution. Learning communities not only provide opportunities for faculty in different, complementary or the same discipline to work together, but they also break down barriers between essential areas of concern bringing, for example, personnel from student affairs and residential life into creative contact with faculty. And, of course, in order to facilitate sustained contact, administrators from all over the college or university find common ground and work together to achieve common goals. As we move forward in higher education, the contribution of the learning community movement might be to insist that new challenges be met with commitments to well-established core values as well as to new ways of fostering student learning and success.

NEW DIRECTIONS FOR TEACHING AND LEARNING • DOI: 10.1002/tl

References

Association of American Colleges and Universities. *College Learning for the New Global Century: A Report from the National Leadership Council for Liberal Education and America's Promise.* Washington, D.C.: AAC&U, 2007.

Boix-Mansilla, V. "Assessing Student Work at Disciplinary Crossroads." *Change: The Magazine of Higher Learning,* 2005, 37(1), 14–21.

Bransford, J. D., Brown, A. L., and Cocking, R. R. (eds.). *How People Learn: Brain, Mind, Experience, and School.* National Research Council Report. Washington, D.C.: National Academies Press, 1999.

Chickering, A. W., and Gamson, Z. F. "Seven Principles of Good Practice in Undergraduate Education." *AAHE Bulletin,* 1987, 39(7), 3–7.

Cross, K. P. *Beyond the Open Door.* San Francisco: Jossey-Bass, 1971.

Dunlap, L., and Sult, L. "Juggling and the Art of the Integrative Assignment." *Journal of Learning Communities Research,* 2009, 3(3), 27–45.

Engstrom, C. "Curricular Learning Communities and Under-prepared Students: Providing a Foundation for Future Success." In J. M. Braxton (ed.), *The Role of the Classroom in College Student Persistence.* New Directions for Teaching and Learning, no. 115. San Francisco: Jossey Bass, 2008.

Engstrom, C., and Tinto, V. *Pathways to Student Success: The Impact of Learning Communities on the Success of Academically Under-prepared College Students.* Final report to the William and Flora Hewlett Foundation, 2007.

Gabelnick, F., MacGregor, J., Matthews, R., and Smith, B. *Learning Communities: Making Connections among Students, Faculty and Disciplines.* New Directions for Teaching and Learning, no. 41. San Francisco: Jossey-Bass, 1990.

Geri, L., Kuehn, D., and MacGregor, J. "From Innovation to Reform: Reflections on Case Studies of 19 Learning Community Initiatives." In J. MacGregor (comp.), *Strengthening Learning Communities: Case Studies from the National Learning Communities Dissemination Project (FIPSE).* Olympia, Wash.: Washington Center for Improving the Quality of Undergraduate Education, The Evergreen State College, 1999.

Hardiman, J., Smith, B. L., Washington, K., and Brewster, E. "Connecting with Local Communities." In B. L. Smith and L. B. Williams, (eds.), *Learning Communities and Student Affairs: Partnering for Powerful Learning.* Learning Communities and Educational Reform, Fall 2007. Olympia, Wash.: Washington Center for Improving the Quality of Undergraduate Education, The Evergreen State College, 2007.

Henscheid, J. M. *Integrating the First-Year Experience: The Role of First-Year Seminars in Learning Communities.* Monograph No. 39. Columbia: National Resource Center for the First-Year Experience and Students in Transition, University of South Carolina, 2004.

Hurd, S., and Stein, R. (eds.). *Building and Sustaining Learning Communities: The Syracuse University Experience.* Boston: Anker Publishing, 2004.

Kuh, G. D. *High-Impact Educational Practices: What They Are, Who Has Access to Them, and Why They Matter.* Washington, D.C.: Association of American Colleges and Universities, 2008.

Lardner, E., and Malnarich, G. "A New Era in Learning Community Work: Why the Pedagogy of Intentional Integration Matters." *Change: The Magazine of Higher Learning.* Jul.–Aug. 2008a, 40(4), 30–37.

Lardner, E. D., and Malnarich, G. "Sustaining Learning Communities: Moving from Curricular to Educational Reform." *Massachusetts Association for Supervision and Curriculum Development Perspectives,* Winter 2008b, 20–23.

MacGregor, J. "Collaborative Learning: Shared Inquiry as a Process of Reform." In M. Svinicki, (ed.), *The Changing Face of College Teaching.* New Directions for Teaching and Learning, no. 42. San Francisco: Jossey-Bass, 1990.

MacGregor, J. (ed.). *Integrating Learning Communities with Service Learning.* National Learning Communities Project Monograph Series. Olympia: Washington Center for Improving the Quality of Undergraduate Education, The Evergreen State College, 2003.

Malnarich, G., and others. *The Pedagogy of Possibilities: Developmental Education, College-Level Studies, and Learning Communities.* National Learning Communities Project Monograph Series. Olympia: Washington Center for Improving the Quality of Undergraduate Education, The Evergreen State College, 2003.

Matthews, R. S. "Collaborative Learning: Creating Knowledge with Students." In R. Menges and M. Weimer (eds.), *Teaching on Solid Ground: Using Scholarship to Improve Practice.* San Francisco: Jossey-Bass, 1995.

Matthews, R. S., Cooper, J., Davidson, N., and Hawkes, P. "Bridging the Gap between Cooperative and Collaborative Learning." *Change: The Magazine of Higher Learning,* Jul.–Aug. 1995, 28(4), 25–39.

Pedersen, S. *Learning Communities and the Academic Library.* National Learning Communities Project Monograph Series. Olympia: Washington Center for Improving the Quality of Undergraduate Education, The Evergreen State College, 2003.

Shapiro, N. S., and Levine, J. *Creating Learning Communities.* San Francisco: Jossey Bass, 1999.

Smith, B. L., and MacGregor, J. "What Is Collaborative Learning?" In A. S. Goodsell and others (eds.), *Collaborative Learning: A Sourcebook for Higher Education.* University Park: National Center on Postsecondary Teaching, Learning and Assessment, Pennsylvania State University, 1992.

Smith, B. L., MacGregor, J., Matthews, R. S., and Gabelnick, F. *Learning Communities: Reforming Undergraduate Education.* San Francisco: Jossey Bass, 2004.

Smith, B. L., Williams, L. B., and others. *Learning Communities and Student Affairs: Partnerships for Powerful Learning.* Learning Communities and Educational Reform, Fall 2007. Olympia: Washington Center for Improving the Quality of Undergraduate Education, The Evergreen State College, 2007.

Taylor, K., Moore, W. S., MacGregor, J., and Lindblad, J. *What We Know Now about Learning Community Research and Assessment.* National Learning Communities Project Monograph Series. Olympia: Washington Center for Improving the Quality of Undergraduate Education, The Evergreen State College, 2003.

Tinto, V. *Leaving College: Rethinking the Causes and Cures of Student Attrition.* Chicago: University of Chicago Press, 1987.

Tinto, V., Goodsell, A., and Russo, P. *Building Learning Communities for New College Students.* University Park: National Center on Postsecondary Teaching, Learning and Assessment, Pennsylvania State University, 1994.

Upcraft, L., and Gardner, J. N. *The Freshman Year Experience: Helping Students Survive and Succeed in College.* San Francisco: Jossey-Bass, 1989.

Visher, M. G., Schneider, E., Wathington, H., and Collado, H. *Scaling Up Learning Communities: The Experience of Six Community Colleges.* National Center for Postsecondary Research, New York, 2010.

ROBERTA S. MATTHEWS *is the senior fellow at the John N. Gardner Institute for Excellence in Undergraduate Education. She also serves as a consultant on higher education issues with a number of colleges and universities.*

BARBARA LEIGH SMITH *is senior scholar and director of the Enduring Legacies Native Case Studies Initiative at the Evergreen State College.*

JEAN MACGREGOR *is a senior scholar at the Washington Center for Improving the Quality of Undergraduate Education at the Evergreen State College, where she directs Curriculum for the Bioregion, a sustainability education initiative involving faculty at colleges and universities in Washington State.*

NEW DIRECTIONS FOR TEACHING AND LEARNING • DOI: 10.1002/tl

INDEX

Appendix
General Learning Community Resources and Examples of Other Discipline-Centered Communities

I. General Resources for Learning Communities in Higher Education

- The Washington Center for Improving the Quality of Under-graduate Education (www.evergreen.edu/washcenter), includes the Learning Communities National Resource Center and offers a summer institute for campus teams.
- The National Learning Communities Conference, sponsored by a consortium of colleges in the midwest: http://nlcc.uc.iupui.edu /nlcc2012/Home.aspx
- The Atlantic Center for Learning Communities is a regional network of LC leaders from a variety of institutions, offering an annual curriculum planning retreat and ongoing communication: www .wagner.edu/aclc

II. Discipline-Centered Learning Communities in Arts and Architecture

- Art Haus Learning Community at Appalachian State University http://housing.appstate.edu/rlc
- Fine Arts Learning Community at University of Connecticut http://lc.uconn.edu/communities/finearts/
- Fine Arts Living Learning Community at the University of Florida http://www.housing.ufl.edu/aie/reid.php
- Fine Arts Learning Community at University of Missouri http://reslife.missouri.edu/tlc#farc
- The Arts Learning Community at James Madison University http://www.jmu.edu/orl/involved/arts.html
- The Arts Initiative Residential Learning Community at the University of Vermont http://www.uvm.edu/~rlc/?Page=airlc/overview.html&SM=airlc /airlc_sm.html
- Music Learning Community at University of Connecticut http://lc.uconn.edu/communities/music/
- Music Learning Community at Iowa State University http://www.music.iastate.edu/org/esprit/
- The Stephenson Towers Living Learning Community at Washington State University http://www.cea.wsu.edu/LLC

- Architecture, Design, and Construction Learning Communities at Auburn University
  http://www.auburn.edu/academic/provost/undergrad_studies/learning_communities/pdf/LC_CatalogBrochure2012.pdf
- Architecture & Design Learning Community at Texas Tech University
  http://housing.ttu.edu/archdesignlc.php

III. Discipline-Centered Learning Communities in Business

- Business Exploration Learning Community at Appalachian State University
  http://housing.appstate.edu/rlc
- Business Learning Community at Auburn University
  http://www.auburn.edu/academic/provost/undergrad_studies/learning_communities/pdf/LC_CatalogBrochure2012.pdf
- Business Connections—A Learning Community for Business Majors at the University of Connecticut
  http://lc.uconn.edu/communities/business/
- Business Learning Community at Drexel University
  http://www.lebow.drexel.edu/Prospects/Undergraduate/BLC/index.php
- Sophomore Business Learning Community at Georgia State University
  http://robinson.gsu.edu/undergraduate/blc.html
- Business Learning Communities at Iowa State University
  http://www.lc.iastate.edu/lc_index.html
- Business Honors Learning Community at the Ohio State University
  http://fisher.osu.edu/undergraduate/future-students/our-program/business-honors-learning-community/
- Residential Business Learning Community at Michigan State University
  http://uas.broad.msu.edu/broad-opportunities/rbp/
- Exploring Business and Economics Learning Community at SUNY Potsdam
  http://www.potsdam.edu/support/firstyear/groups/business.cfm
- Business Management Learning Communities at Syracuse University
  http://lc.syr.edu/future-students/which-one/business-management.html
- Business Learning Community at University of Nebraska
  http://cba.unl.edu/students/prospective/blc.aspx
- Belk College Business Learning Community at University of North Carolina (UNC) Charlotte
  http://blc.uncc.edu/

IV. Discipline-Centered Learning Communities in Education

- Future Educators Learning Community at Appalachian State University
  http://housing.appstate.edu/rlc
- Education Learning Community at Auburn University
  http://www.auburn.edu/academic/provost/undergrad_studies/learning_communities/pdf/LC_CatalogBrochure2012.pdf
- Preparing Tomorrow's Teachers Learning Community at Iowa State University
  http://www.lc.iastate.edu/directories/PT2.html
- Teacher Education Learning Community at James Madison University
  http://www.jmu.edu/orl/involved/roop.html
- Education Learning Communities at Purdue University
  http://www.purdue.edu/sats/learning_communities/profiles/education/index.html
- Education Learning Community at SUNY Potsdam
  http://www.potsdam.edu/support/firstyear/groups/Childhood-Early-Childhood-Education.cfm
- Education Learning Community at Syracuse University
  http://lc.syr.edu/future-students/which-one/communities/ellc.html
- Education Learning Community at University of Missouri
  http://reslife.missouri.edu/tlc#education
- Education Learning Community I & II at Wayne State University
  http://coe.wayne.edu/learning-communities/intro-to-education.php

V. Discipline-Centered Learning Communities in Health and Medicine

- Allied Medical Professions Learning Community at Ohio State University
  http://urds.osu.edu/learningcommunities/allied-medical-professions-learning-community/
- Exploring Medicine Learning Community at University of Nebraska
  http://www.unl.edu/learncom/exploring-medicine
- Food Science and Human Nutrition Learning Community at Iowa State University
  http://www.lc.iastate.edu/lc_index.html
- Pre-Health Learning Community at Auburn University
  http://www.auburn.edu/academic/cosam/departments/student-services/learning-communities.htm
- Key Health Professions Learning Community at Colorado State University
  http://keyhp.lc.colostate.edu/new-page.aspx

- Health Professions Learning Community at University of Illinois
  http://www.housing.illinois.edu/Current/Living-Learning/Health
  %20Professions/Academics.aspx
- Pre-professional Health Learning Community at James Madison
  University
  http://www.jmu.edu/orl/involved/huber.html
- Health Studies Learning Community at Saint Louis University
  http://www.slu.edu/x27202.xml
- Health Studies Learning Community at Syracuse University
  http://lc.syr.edu/future-students/which-one/communities/health
  -studies.html
- Health and Exercise Science Learning Community at Syracuse
  University
  http://lc.syr.edu/future-students/which-one/communities/health
  -exercise-science.html
- Health Connections Learning Community at UNC Charlotte
  http://coe.uncc.edu/flc/
- Health Sciences Learning Community at University of Michigan
  http://www.lsa.umich.edu/hssp/
- Pre-Medical Learning Community at Miami University
  http://www.units.muohio.edu/saf/reslife/reslife/livingatmiami
  /mwph/mwph.php
- Pharmacy Learning Community at Ohio State University
  http://urds.osu.edu/learningcommunities/pharmacy-house-learning
  -community/
- Pre-Pharmacy Learning Community at University of Connecticut
  http://lc.uconn.edu/communities/pharm/
- Nursing Learning Community at Auburn University
  http://www.auburn.edu/academic/provost/undergrad_studies
  /learning_communities/pdf/LC_CatalogBrochure2012.pdf
- Nursing Learning Community at Ohio State University
  http://urds.osu.edu/learningcommunities/nursing-learning
  -community/
- Nursing Learning Community at University of Connecticut
  http://lc.uconn.edu/communities/nursing/
- Pre-Vet Learning Community at Auburn University
  http://www.auburn.edu/academic/provost/undergrad_studies
  /learning_communities/pdf/LC_CatalogBrochure2012.pdf

VI. Discipline-Centered Learning Communities in the Humanities

- Arts and Humanities Learning Community at Michigan State
  University
  http://rcah.msu.edu/
- Arts and Letters Learning Community at Elon University
  http://www.elon.edu/e-web/students/reslife/artsandletters.xhtml

- Humanities Learning Community at Kent State University
  http://www.kent.edu/cas/rescollege/learningcommunities/humanities
  .cfm
- Humanities Learning Community at San Francisco State University
  http://www.sfsu.edu/~housing/learningcom/index.html#
- Humanities House, A Learning Community at the University of
  Connecticut
  http://lc.uconn.edu/communities/humanities/
- Language and Culture Learning Communities at Ithaca College
  http://www.ithaca.edu/hs/depts/mll/langcommun/
- Languages, Cultures, and Arts Learning Community at Syracuse
  University
  http://lc.syr.edu/future-students/which-one/communities/lca.html
- Creative Nonfiction Learning Community at Syracuse University
  http://lc.syr.edu/future-students/which-one/communities
  /creative-nonfiction.html
- Poetry Arts Learning Community at Syracuse University
  http://lc.syr.edu/future-students/which-one/communities/poets
  .html

VII. Discipline-Centered Learning Communities in Science, Technology,
Engineering, and Math (STEM)

- Biology Learning Community at James Madison University
  http://www.jmu.edu/orl/involved/trelawney.html
- Biology Learning Community at University of Nebraska
  http://www.unl.edu/learncom/biology
- Biochemistry and Biophysics Learning Community at Iowa State
  University
  http://www.lc.iastate.edu/directories/BBLC.html
- Conservation Biology, Marine Biology, and Microbiology Learning
  Communities at Auburn University
  http://www.auburn.edu/academic/cosam/departments/student
  -services/learning-communities.htm
- Chemistry Learning Community at Iowa State University
  http://www.chem.iastate.edu/undergrad/learning-community.html
- Computer Science Learning Community at Iowa State University
  http://www.cs.iastate.edu/community/LC.shtml
- Computer Science Learning Community at the University of Texas
  Dallas
  http://www.utdallas.edu/livinglearning/computerscience/
- Engineering Learning Community at Auburn University
  http://www.auburn.edu/academic/provost/undergrad_studies
  /learning_communities/pdf/LC_CatalogBrochure2012.pdf

- Engineering Learning Community at the University of Connecticut
  http://lc.uconn.edu/communities/engineering/
- Engineering Learning Community at Drexel University
  http://drexel.edu/engineering/resources/prosp_students/elc/
- Engineering Learning Communities at Iowa State University
  http://www.lc.iastate.edu/lc_index.html
- Engineering Learning Communities at IUPUI
  http://tlc.iupui.edu/TLCPrograms/TLCThemesDescriptions
  .aspx
- Engineering Learning Community at UNC Charlotte
  http://coe.uncc.edu/flc/
- Engineering Learning Community at Purdue University
  https://engineering.purdue.edu/ENE/Academics/FirstYear/lc
- Engineering Learning Community at Rutgers University
  http://rulc.rutgers.edu/content/engineering-living-learning
  -community
- L. C. Smith College of Engineering and Computer Science (LCS)
  Learning Community at Syracuse University
  http://lc.syr.edu/future-students/which-one/communities/lcs
  -engineering.html
- Engineering Learning Community at Texas A&M
  http://reslife.tamu.edu/housing/llc/engineer.asp
- Environmental Science Learning Community at Iowa State
  University
  http://www.ensci.iastate.edu/undergrad/prostudents/lc.htm
- Genetics Learning Community at Iowa State University
  http://www.public.iastate.edu/~ugradgen/LCHome.shtml
- Life Sciences Learning Community at Saint Louis University
  http://www.slu.edu/x27201.xml
- Science, Technology, and Math Learning Community at Syracuse
  University
  http://lc.syr.edu/future-students/which-one/communities/science
  -tech-math.html
- Women in Science and Engineering Learning Community at
  Auburn University
  http://www.auburn.edu/academic/provost/undergrad_studies
  /learning_communities/pdf/LC_CatalogBrochure2012.pdf
- Women in Science and Engineering Learning Community at the
  University of Wisconsin
  http://www.housing.wisc.edu/wise
- Women in Math, Science, and Engineering Learning Community at
  the University of Connecticut
  http://lc.uconn.edu/communities/wimse/
- Women in Math, Science, and Engineering Learning Community at
  the University of Illinois

NEW DIRECTIONS FOR TEACHING AND LEARNING • DOI: 10.1002/tl

http://www.housing.illinois.edu/Housing/Current/Living-Learning
/WIMSE.aspx
- Women in Science Disciplines, Engineering and Math Learning
Community at Miami University
http://www.units.muohio.edu/saf/reslife/reslife/livingatmiami
/WIMSE/WIMSE.php
- Women in Engineering Learning Community at Ohio State
University
http://urds.osu.edu/learningcommunities/women-in-engineering
-learning-community/
- Thinking through Computing
http://support.csis.pace.edu/CSISWeb/docs/techReports/techReport
221.pdf

VIII. Discipline-Centered Learning Communities in the Social Sciences

- Anthropology Learning Community at Iowa State University
http://www.lc.iastate.edu/directories/aaa.html
- Social Science and Public Policy Living-Learning Community at
Florida State University
http://publicaffairsllc.fsu.edu/
- Social Science Learning Community at Kent State University
http://www.kent.edu/cas/rescollege/learningcommunities
/socialscience.cfm
- Global Village Learning Community at UNC Charlotte
http://sociology.uncc.edu/Undergraduate/global-village-learning
-community.html
- Social Science Researchers (Race and Ethnicity) Living Learning
Community at the University of Pittsburgh
http://www.studentaffairs.pitt.edu/reslifesocialsciencellc

NEW DIRECTIONS FOR TEACHING AND LEARNING

ORDER FORM SUBSCRIPTION AND SINGLE ISSUES

DISCOUNTED BACK ISSUES:

Use this form to receive 20% off all back issues of *New Directions for Teaching and Learning*.
All single issues priced at **$23.20** (normally $29.00)

TITLE	ISSUE NO.	ISBN

Call 888-378-2537 or see mailing instructions below. When calling, mention the promotional code JBNND to receive your discount. For a complete list of issues, please visit www.josseybass.com/go/ndtl

SUBSCRIPTIONS: (1 YEAR, 4 ISSUES)

☐ New Order ☐ Renewal

U.S.	☐ Individual: $89	☐ Institutional: $292
CANADA/MEXICO	☐ Individual: $89	☐ Institutional: $332
ALL OTHERS	☐ Individual: $113	☐ Institutional: $366

Call 888-378-2537 or see mailing and pricing instructions below.
Online subscriptions are available at www.onlinelibrary.wiley.com

ORDER TOTALS:

Issue / Subscription Amount: $ _____

Shipping Amount: $ _____
(for single issues only – subscription prices include shipping)

Total Amount: $ _____

SHIPPING CHARGES:

First Item	$6.00
Each Add'l Item	$2.00

(No sales tax for U.S. subscriptions. Canadian residents, add GST for subscription orders. Individual rate subscriptions must be paid by personal check or credit card. Individual rate subscriptions may not be resold as library copies.)

BILLING & SHIPPING INFORMATION:

☐ **PAYMENT ENCLOSED:** *(U.S. check or money order only. All payments must be in U.S. dollars.)*

☐ **CREDIT CARD:** ☐ VISA ☐ MC ☐ AMEX

Card number _____ Exp. Date _____

Card Holder Name_____ Card Issue # _____

Signature _____ Day Phone _____

☐ **BILL ME:** *(U.S. institutional orders only. Purchase order required.)*

Purchase order # _____
Federal Tax ID 13559302 • GST 89102-8052

Name _____

Address_____

Phone_____ E-mail_____

Copy or detach page and send to: **John Wiley & Sons, One Montgomery Street, Suite 1200, San Francisco, CA 94104-4594**

Order Form can also be faxed to: **888-481-2665**

PROMO JBNND

Statement of Ownership

Statement of Ownership, Management, and Circulation (required by 39 U.S.C. 3685), filed on OCTOBER 1, 2012, for NEW DIRECTIONS FOR TEACHING AND LEARNING (Publication No. 0271-0633), published quarterly for an annual subscription price of $89 at Wiley Subscription Services, Inc., at Jossey-Bass, One Montgomery St., Suite 1200, San Francisco, CA 94104-4594.

The names and complete mailing addresses of the Publisher, Editor, and Managing Editor are: Publisher, Wiley Subscription Services, Inc., A Wiley Company at San Francisco, One Montgomery St., Suite 1200, San Francisco, CA 94104-4594; Editor, Catherine M. Wehlburg, TCU Box 297028, Texas Christian University, Fort Worth, TX 76129; Managing Editor, None, . Contact Person: Joe Schuman; Telephone: 415-782-3232.

NEW DIRECTIONS FOR TEACHING AND LEARNING is a publication owned by Wiley Subscription Services, Inc. The known bondholders, mortgagees, and other security holders owning or holding 1% or more of total amount of bonds, mortgages, or other securities are (see list).

	Average No. Copies Each Issue During Preceding 12 Months	No. Copies Of Single Issue Published Nearest To Filing Date (Summer 2012)
15a. Total number of copies (net press run)	941	837
15b. Legitimate paid and/or requested distribution (by mail and outside mail)		
15b(1). Individual paid/requested mail subscriptions stated on PS form 3541 (include direct written request from recipient, telemarketing, and Internet requests from recipient, paid subscriptions including nominal rate subscriptions, advertiser's proof copies, and exchange copies)	339	314
15b(2). Copies requested by employers for distribution to employees by name or position, stated on PS form 3541	0	0
15b(3). Sales through dealers and carriers, street vendors, counter sales, and other paid or requested distribution outside USPS	0	0
15b(4). Requested copies distributed by other mail classes through USPS	0	0
15c. Total paid and/or requested circulation (sum of 15b(1), (2), (3), and (4))	339	314
15d. Nonrequested distribution (by mail and outside mail)		
15d(1). Outside county nonrequested copies stated on PS form 3541	11	8
15d(2). In-county nonrequested copies stated on PS form 3541	0	0
15d(3). Nonrequested copies distributed through the USPS by other classes of mail	0	0
15d(4). Nonrequested copies distributed outside the mail	0	0
15e. Total nonrequested distribution (sum of 15d(1), (2), (3), and (4))	11	8
15f. Total distribution (sum of 15c and 15e)	350	322
15g. Copies not distributed	591	515
15h. Total (sum of 15f and 15g)	941	837
15i. Percent paid and/or requested circulation (15c divided by 15f times 100)	96.8%	97.6%

I certify that all information furnished on this form is true and complete. I understand that anyone who furnishes false or misleading information on this form or who omits material or information requested on this form may be subject to criminal sanctions (including fines and imprisonment) and/or civil sanctions (including civil penalties).

Statement of Ownership will be printed in the Winter 2012 issue of this publication.

(signed) Susan E. Lewis, VP & Publisher-Periodicals